16 Messages For An Election Year

The Platform Of Jesus

Lowell Messerschmidt

CSS Publishing Co., Inc., Lima, Ohio

16 MESSAGES FOR AN ELECTION YEAR

Second Printing 2008

Copyright © 1992 by
CSS Publishing Company, Inc.
Lima, Ohio

All rights reserved. No part of this publication may be reproduced in any manner whatsoever without the prior permission of the publisher, except in the case of brief quotations embodied in critical articles and reviews. Inquiries should be addressed to: Permissions, CSS Publishing Company, Inc., 517 South Main Street, Lima, Ohio 45804.

Scripture quotations are from the Revised Standard Version of the Bible, copyrighted 1946, 1952 (c), 1971, 1973, by the Division of Christian Education of the National Council of the Churches of Christ in the USA. Used by permission.

Scripture quotations marked (KJV) are from the King James Version of the Bible, in the public domain.

Library of Congress Cataloging-in-Publication Data

Messerschmidt, Lowell.
   16 messages for an election year : the platform of Jesus / by Lowell Messerschmidt.
     p.cm.
   ISBN 1-55673-398-4
   1. Jesus Christ—Biography—Public life—Sermons. 2. Sermons, American. I. Title.

BT306.3.M471992
252'.68—dc20
                                                   91-39300
                                                        CIP

For more information about CSS Publishing Company resources, visit our website at www.csspub.com or email us at csr@csspub.com or call (800) 241-4056.

Cover design by Barbara Spencer
ISBN-13: 978-1-55673-398-7
ISBN-10: 1-55673-398-4   PRINTED IN USA

To
Our Daughters
Who Have Brought Great Joy
To Our Family
Carol
Susan
Ruth
Linda
Nancy
Julie

Table Of Contents

Chapter 1
    Jesus Announces His Platform   7

Chapter 2
    Jesus' Campaign Strategy   13

Chapter 3
    Jesus' Whistle-stop Campaign   19

Chapter 4
    Concerning The Nature And Destiny Of Humankind   25

Chapter 5
    Concerning The Kingdom Of God   31

Chapter 6
    Concerning The Church   37

Chapter 7
    Concerning The Unity Of Christians   43

Chapter 8
    Concerning Prayer   47

Chapter 9
    Concerning Forgiveness   53

Chapter 10
    Concerning Possessions And Money Matters   59

Chapter 11
    Concerning Suffering   65

Chapter 12
    Concerning Love   71

Chapter 13
  Concerning Life After Death   75

Chapter 14
  Concerning The First Coming Of Christ   81

Chapter 15
  Concerning The Second Coming Of Christ   87

Chapter 16
  How Do You Vote?   93

Chapter 1

Jesus Announces His Platform

The Spirit of the Lord is upon me, because he has appointed me to preach good news to the poor. He has sent me to proclaim release to the captives and recovering of sight to the blind, to set at liberty those who are oppressed, to proclaim the acceptable year of the Lord. — Isaiah 61:1-2; Luke 4:18-19

While the traditional day for the beginning of a presidential campaign is Labor Day, there usually is so much political activity for the previous months, that all traditional dates have lost their meaning. During the ensuing campaign, the candidates set forth some of the programs in which they say they believe, and presumably will try to enact if elected.

In the scriptures we find that early in Jesus' public ministry he, too, announced a platform. While he did not spell out just what he meant in every detail, we find that Jesus set forth the principles that were to guide his ministry. It is apparent that no one could exactly foresee what direction this would take which, in Jesus' case, led to the cross. It is significant that he enunciated these principles at the start of his ministry.

As Luke records Jesus' life, he gives us a preface to Jesus' announcement: the story of the vision that came to Mary, the birth and background of John the Baptist, the beautiful story of Jesus' birth, some of the preaching of John, the baptism and genealogy of Jesus, and the temptations of Jesus.

Immediately following the temptations, Jesus came to his hometown, Nazareth, to preach his inaugural sermon. This sermon contained the program of his ministry.

Today, Nazareth appears to be a little more than a fair-sized village. In the ancient world it was probably much larger. The ancient Greeks referred to it as a polis, a city. Some scholars estimate it may have had as many as 20,000 inhabitants. From the nearby hills one could see the sites of many of the important happenings of the Old Testament. Surely Jesus had not only the scriptures to learn, but the advantage of living in the area where the history of the scriptures had been made. Great trade routes ran close to Nazareth. Because Jesus was reared in a town with history passing its gates, he was not ignorant of the affairs of the world.

On this occasion, Jesus went into the synagogue on the sabbath, as was his custom. He was given a scroll by the *chazzan* who was in charge of the scrolls of the synagogue. The *chazzan*'s work consisted of taking the scrolls from the cabinet and, after their use, returning them for safekeeping. He also was to keep the synagogue clean. It was his responsibility to announce the coming of the sabbath with three blasts of the silver trumpet from the synagogue roof. He was the teacher of the village school. After receiving the scroll, Jesus read from chapter 61 of the prophet Isaiah: "The Spirit of the Lord is upon me, because he has anointed me to preach good news to the poor. He has sent me to proclaim release to the captives and recovering of sight to the blind, to set at liberty those who are oppressed, to proclaim the acceptable year of the Lord" (Isaiah 61:1-2; Luke 4:18-19).

Jesus declared that he came to bring total salvation to people. The noun for "salvation" is *soteria* in the Greek. The verb, "to save," is *sozein*. When this is used, it means both to save a man in the eternal sense, and to heal a man in the physical sense. New Testament salvation has a much broader base than is often given by some Christians. Some limit salvation to what they call the soul; there is little or no salvation for all of society and for all human relationships. This was not Jesus' view of salvation; he looked at salvation as encompassing all of life.

The writer of the passage from Isaiah quoted by Jesus does not call himself a servant but the ideas he expressed are much the same as in the several "servant" passages that one finds earlier in Isaiah (Isaiah 42:1-4; 49:1-6; 50:1-9; 52:13—53:12). He was speaking in the confused and chaotic years of which eight followed the return of the Hebrews from the period of exile in Babylon. Those were years that brought mis-government, poverty, and moral disintegration to those who had come back with great hopes for the future. The people were wretched, physically and spiritually. They needed good tidings as much as did their relatives who had spent years in exile in Babylon. Unfilled hopes brought frustration.

The conditions in the time of Jesus were similar. The hopes and fears of all the years were present in those days. Jesus could quote from the Isaiah passages, knowing he was not only speaking to the problem the people faced, but also implying that he was the servant who could help them. This was intensified by Jesus claiming "the spirit of the Lord is upon me." He then announced his platform that spoke to the complete needs of humankind.

"He has anointed me to preach good news to the poor." Jesus used this on other occasions as well. When Jesus stated his credentials to John the Baptist's disciples who asked if he was the anointed one, Jesus said, "The poor have the gospel preached to them." In the first beatitude, he said, "Blessed are the poor in spirit."

The use of this word does not mean merely honest poverty and the struggle of one trying to make a living. It describes abject poverty, which has nothing and places a person in danger of real starvation. It describes acute destitution. Jesus was saying he was anointed or sent or commissioned to preach good news to all who were spiritually destitute.

This good news to the poor was a spiritual message by which Jesus linked the present life to the life after death. He preached a message in which he was trying to spiritualize all the normal activities of life. Here is the promise of good news to people who cannot see the connection between their normal activities of life and God.

"He has sent me to proclaim release to the captives ... to set at liberty those who are oppressed." Jesus was giving a spiritual dimension to social problems. Many of the great crusades for freedom have been carried on by followers of Christ. In the latter part of the eighteenth and first part of the nineteenth centuries a group of evangelicals, often members of the Church of England, led the battle against slavery. The most famous was Wilbur Wilberforce who led the fight in Parliament for the law which, in 1807, abolished the slave trade in the British Empire. Associated with him was Thomas Clarkson, a clergyman's son, who had planned to follow his father's profession but changed his mind and devoted himself to the anti-slavery crusade. In the name of Christ they were proclaiming release to the captives.

There is also the imprisonment of sin and of fear. There is the captivity of the flesh because one yields more to his or her appetites and passions until finally he is a slave to dissipation and degradation. Jesus calls all from that kind of activity, challenging them to purity and offering them the power by which they can cut the chains that bind them.

There is also the captivity of discouragement and disorganization in life. Many feel inadequate and frustrated. They feel they cannot work out a meaningful destiny of their own. Such captivities degrade the human soul. To all of these Jesus felt it his purpose to set men free.

"He has sent me to proclaim ... recovering of sight to the blind." Jesus is speaking in terms both spiritual and medical. He always emphasized that there was a spiritual blindness to which all are susceptible. He told the Pharisees that if they were not so blind, they could see. In this instance he was not speaking of the health of the eye, but of spiritual health.

Jesus spent much of his time and energy in healing those who were physically sick. He did this, not because those healed necessarily became his followers, but because he wanted them to be whole. The third gospel tells of 24 instances of healing by Jesus. In only about one-fourth of those instances is faith mentioned. Jesus did not believe he should bargain for followers by healing them. Healing was an end in itself.

The good news of Christ, which has been preached by his church through the years has included the healing of physical bodies. Look at the directory of hospitals in almost any city. Many, in some cities the only, hospital is there because of the Church of Christ. Or, if you will, listen to the story of Amy Skartved who was a missionary nurse in Nigeria:

> *I was called about ten o'clock one night to see a lad who had been taken ill suddenly with cerebral malaria. He was in a coma and I had little hope of saving the*

lad's life. After giving him heart stimulants and malarial treatment by injection, I stayed with the family until the boy showed some improvement, praying that God would heal the lad. At three o'clock in the morning, when I was called for a delivery, I checked on the boy again and found him sleeping quietly. Again, with thanks to him who is always near, I was grateful for the privilege of welcoming a newborn babe into the world.

Along with a full medical program is the care of a twin born prematurely and weighing less than two and one-half pounds at birth. The mother has one living child, followed by three abortions in which the children have all died, being too small to live. One of the twins died the day after birth, but the other is doing well so far. I am hoping this one will live.[1]

"The Spirit of the Lord is upon me ... to proclaim the acceptable year of the Lord." The other goals would only become a reality if people committed their lives to God. The acceptable years of the Lord would only be a reality if people looked upon it as ever present, but also something that was to come. God is in control of the universe, now and forever.

After Jesus read these portions from Isaiah, he sat down. This did not mean he was finished. This meant he was able to start because the speaker always gave his address seated, and rabbis taught sitting down in a way that reminds us of the phrase, "the professor's chair."

At first, all spoke well of him. After all, this was a person who had been reared in the community. There was probably a sense of pride among the people as they listened to a person whose parents were a part of the community.

Then Jesus said that his platform was not only for them, but for people everywhere, even the non-Jews in Sidon and Syria. Their attitude changed. Now they did not think so well of him. They drove him from the synagogue and tried to kill him by throwing him down a precipice. But Jesus, in his masterful way, walked through the crowd and went his way. No one touched him.

The gospel was described as foolishness by Saint Paul. Surely Jesus' announcement of his platform and his exposition was foolishness. If he wanted "votes," he seems to have lost most of them that day in Nazareth. This shows that no one should ever try to equate the gospel with a popularity contest. The gospel is not intended to be popular. It is intended to save people. It is designed to do this for people of all backgrounds. Jesus proclaimed this in his platform.

---

1. Amy Skartved in *World Evangel*, Dayton, Ohio, March, 1960.

Chapter 2

Jesus' Campaign Strategy

All authority in heaven and on earth has been given to me. Go therefore and make disciples of all nations, baptizing them in the name of the Father and of the Son and of the Holy Spirit, teaching them to observe all that I have commanded you; and lo, I am with you always, to the end of the age. — Matthew 28:18-20

When political parties in the United States plan their campaign strategies, they emphasize certain issues in various parts of the country and de-emphasize those issues in other sections. Farm issues take precedence in the Midwest and industrial issues are emphasized in areas of manufacturing.

Jesus also had his campaign strategy. It was unlike that of most political parties. In fact, Jesus never announced a strategy. It was not until his last days on earth that he revealed his campaign strategy. By that time he had already experienced what seemed complete defeat by a landslide. But, a few days later, after the resurrection, it appeared that the first vote had been wrong, and he was declared a winner, at least by those who knew him by faith. It was then that he announced his strategy.

To announce the strategy after, rather than before the campaign, seems senseless in human terms. It is another example where the foolishness of God is wiser than humans.

It was near the end of his days on earth that Jesus declared to his disciples, "All authority in heaven and on earth has been given to me. Go therefore, and make disciples of all nations, baptizing them in the name of the Father, and of the Son and of the Holy Spirit, teaching them to observe all that I have commanded you and lo, I am with you always, to the close of the age" (Matthew 28:18-20). A short time later he directed his followers to carry a witness for him into every precinct in the world, even where the voters were presumably disenfranchised, such as in Samaria.

While he did not announce his strategy at first, with hindsight we see that he did have a plan during his earthly ministry. He organized an inner circle of assistants, only twelve in number. On another occasion he sent seventy of his followers as an advance team to places where he himself was about to go, to prepare the way for him. It appears that his strategy was not necessarily to win great numbers, but to win committed people who would submit themselves to the disciplines of God.

As we consider Jesus' campaign strategy, we see that Jesus was utterly honest in his campaign speeches. He did not "trim his sails" to get votes. He did not say one thing in Judea, another thing in Samaria, and other things in Galilee, all contradictory, in order to win votes in those places. His message was universal and would apply everywhere.

There were times that Jesus appeared to be alienating voters. One man asked Jesus to help divide his inheritance. Jesus had an opportunity to be helpful and gain support. It was a chance for Jesus to gain some popularity. Instead, Jesus asked the man to tell him who made him a judge in such instances, and told the story of a rich fool.

The honesty of Jesus can be seen further in his condemnation of various places. Can anyone imagine an American presidential candidate condemning or denouncing Chicago or Dallas or Los Angeles for the wickedness of those cities? But, listen to Jesus: "Woe to you, Chorazin! woe to you, Bethsaida! ... And you, Capernaum, will you be exalted in heaven? You shall be brought down to Hades" (Matthew 20:21-23).

Paul Douglas was a Chicago alderman before he became a United States Senator from Illinois. While an alderman, a woman and her young daughter came to him one afternoon. The mother had entered her daughter in a tap dancing contest but the daughter did not know how to tap dance. Alderman Douglas spent a couple of hours trying to teach the girl to tap dance. Such are among the experiences of an American politician.

Jesus was nakedly honest with the rich young ruler. The man wanted to follow Jesus on his own terms, not those of Jesus. But Jesus told him to sell what he had and give it to the poor. The man refused to do it, and went away sorrowful. Jesus did not compromise in order to gain a convert, or to gain a vote. By modern political thinking, this was poor campaign strategy.

On occasion, it seems Jesus was inviting people to go away. It is obvious he did not try to solicit the votes of the Sadducees and Pharisees, the two most powerful political parties in the state of Judea. Calling people hypocrites is not conducive to winning support. Further, he declared, "Not all who say to me, 'Lord, Lord,' will enter the kingdom of heaven, but those who do the will of my father who is in heaven" (Matthew 7:21). He was honest in pointing out that there would be judgments on all people. The worthless servant who did not care for the talents given him was cast into outer darkness. The one who did not show charity to others would go to eternal punishment.

Jesus' honesty compelled him to hold before the people the fact that to follow him was a costly business. When many people seemed to follow him, he reminded them that if any of them wanted to build a tower, they first would sit down and count the cost because if it was not finished, others would laugh at them. He said that if a king was going to war, he would first count whether his resources were sufficient to give him a good chance of defeating the opposing army. He suggested that anyone who was interested in following him should first count the cost.

He realized it would be costly for him, too. He did not try to hide this fact. "The son of man will be delivered into the hands of men, and they will kill him; and when he is killed, after three days he will rise" (Mark 9:31). While this was not an optimistic promise for himself, he also told his followers, "They will deliver you up to tribulation, and put you to death; and you will be hated by all nations for my name's sake" (Matthew 24:9). Jesus did not try to acquire followers by double-talk. He spoke directly and without compromise.

Jesus' campaign strategy contained a message for all people. When he talked to an outcast woman at Jacob's well in Samaria, even his own followers were amazed. People came to him from the foreign nations of Tyre and Sidon. He visited the Decapolis that was Greek in culture, cities despised by good Jews. He healed the son of a Roman officer.

Jesus' last words were commands to witness for him everywhere. This statement emphasized one he made as he was pointing out the cost of being one of his disciples: "This gospel of the kingdom will be preached through the whole world, as a testimony to all nations" (Matthew 24:14).

Jesus' campaign strategy was for the people of every race; he wanted people of all backgrounds to vote for him as candidates today desire every state to vote for them.

Jesus called and calls dedicated people to his cause. The first people Jesus called were the men whom we call the disciples: Peter, John, and the others. These became district managers. This was true in a real way in later years when they divided and, according to tradition, each one went to some part of the world carrying the gospel. Jesus, however, needed more. We know how he sent out the seventy. Since that day there have been others. Perhaps "ward heelers" is too harsh a term. Instead, "precinct captains" would be more appropriate. Jesus needs those. They are the people who do the footwork. They are the ones who in the name of Christ console the sick, visit those in prison, feed the hungry, and clothe the needy. Their names are seldom known except in heaven. They are the ones who visit the stranger in the community and invite him to church. They are the ones who do all the menial tasks about which few others are aware.

These are the dedicated people; they have to be because, as Jesus pointed out, the cross is a part of their lives. They are the ones to whom the proclamation of the gospel of the kingdom is more important than anything else. They are those who want the church to go forward, who want people to know of Christ, and who are willing to dedicate themselves and their means to that end.

They can be found in Mexico where many churches are in desperate need of a pastor. For years, no stewardship had been taught to converts. Now some major denominations are telling the mission churches that when ten people in that congregation tithe, it will receive its own pastor, with the assumption it will be self-supporting. The church goes forward with dedicated people.

The church in Korea is one of the fastest growing churches in the world. Some congregations are starting in the mountains with a pastor and only a few members. Often these small congregations do not have the resources to pay the pastor an adequate salary. However, larger congregations are voluntarily supplementing the low salaries until the mission congregation can be self-sustaining.

Christ's strategy depends on people on the ward level, on the level of the local church, who are dedicated to achieving his victory. Each person who claims to be a follower must gear his or her life to Christ's strategy. Jesus' strategy was to win the world. Each follower must decide to be a help or a hindrance.

Chapter 3

Jesus' Whistle-stop Campaign

The people sought him and came to him ... but he said to them, "I must preach the good news of the kingdom of God to the other cities also; for I was sent for this purpose." — Luke 4:42-43

He went all about Galilee, teaching in their synagogues and preaching the gospel of the kingdom and healing every disease and every infirmity among the people. So his fame spread throughout all Syria, and they brought him all the sick ... and paralytics, and he healed them.
— Matthew 4:23-24

Candidates for the presidency have elaborate plans. A staff with experience in politics is created to guide the candidate at every step. Great amounts of money are gathered to help with the tremendous expenses of the campaign. Years ago one presidential candidate vowed to visit every state during the campaign. Much of the travel was done by train, with the candidate appearing on the back platform from which he would speak to the crowds. This was the real meaning of the whistle-stop campaign.

It is easy for us to bypass the idea that Jesus also conducted a whistle-stop campaign. Obviously there were no trains. There is no record of Jesus traveling any way but walking, except when he rode a donkey into Jerusalem on what we know as Palm Sunday.

When we read the story of Jesus' life, we learn that as a small babe his parents took him to Egypt to escape the fury of Herod. On one occasion he visited the area of Syro-Phoenecia, which is the southern part of present-day Lebanon. His activities centered on the regions of Galilee, the Decapolis, Samaria, and Judea. This was a very small area. It is said that 90% of the biblical story takes place in an area fifty miles wide and 150 miles long.

Chapter 4 of the gospel of Matthew tells us, "He went about all Galilee, teaching in their synagogues and preaching the gospel of the kingdom and healing every disease and every infirmity among the people. So his fame spread through all Syria, and they brought him all the sick, those afflicted with various diseases and pains, demoniacs, epileptics and paralytics, and he healed them" (Matthew 4:23-24). Reading further, we are told that great crowds followed him from Galilee and the Decapolis and Jerusalem and Judea and from beyond the Jordan.

Many of the places where Jesus stopped were so insignificant that they are remembered only because he stopped there on a particular occasion. That was true of Cana where he attended a wedding. It was true of Bethlehem, Sidon, Nazareth, Capernaum, Bethsaida, and others. The only really significant city that he visited according to the values of that day was Jerusalem.

Wherever he went, Jesus proclaimed good news to the people who came to hear him. That good news was more than campaign oratory as one American presidential candidate described his campaign speeches some years after he met defeat at the hands of the voters. Jesus' good news was something that reached the hearts of those who listened to him with faith. It was especially good news for those who were afflicted with diseases of many kinds for, we are told, he healed them. So effective was he that great crowds followed him wherever he went.

As we consider Jesus' whistle-stop campaign, we must realize he was seeking votes by urging the people to accept the kingdom of God in their lives. This process of acceptance of the kingdom is known as conversion. He emphasized this as a necessity if one was to follow him. He declared, "Except ye be converted, and become as little children, ye shall not enter into the kingdom of heaven" (Matthew 18:3 KJV). To one of the most respected men in the city of Jerusalem, he declared, "Unless one is born anew, he cannot see the kingdom of God" (John 3:3). In many ways and on many occasions, Jesus told people that their lives must undergo a revolution if they were to be his disciples and experience God's kingdom in their lives. They must think differently than previously; their hearts must have a new warmth; their spirits must be quickened and more sensitive; their views of social needs must be sharpened. A definite change was necessary. Mere reform was not enough.

This reflects itself in all of life. Dr. T. R. Glover tells of an agnostic friend who undertook to save a drunkard in order to prove that a person's habits could be transformed without the aid of religion. The man was so weak that he was unable to pass a tavern unless someone had hold of his arm. If his guardian went to London for a day, he immediately went out and became drunk. One day, Dr. Glover met the agnostic and asked about the drunken friend. "Oh," was the reply, "I was getting along fairly well with the job when a lot of rough people with red jerseys arrived with an atrocious brass band. Somehow these repulsive fellows got hold of him. I don't know exactly what happened, but they seemed to have him kneel down and pray. Anyhow, he can walk past a tavern by himself now." His heightened moral powers bear witness to the fact that Christ now controlled his life.

Jesus was interested in what people thought of him. On one occasion he asked a few of the disciples who people said he was. They responded that some of the people said he was John the Baptist or Elijah or Jeremiah or one of the prophets. When he asked the disciples, Peter said, "You are the Christ, the Son of the living God" (Matthew 16:16). This was the correct answer, but Jesus did not respond as most candidates when they are acclaimed as the savior of the political realm. Most candidates wave an appreciative hand. But Jesus told Peter and the rest to tell no one that he was the Christ.

We also find that Jesus did not offer an easy platform. He did not trim his platform in order to suit everyone. Since his platform was from God, he did not seek advice from others how to please the most people. He declared, "When you have lifted up the Son of man, then you will know that I am he, and that I can do nothing on my own authority but speak thus as the Father has taught me" (John 8:28). This idea was further expressed when he said, "This is the work of God, that you believe in him whom he has sent ... For I have come down from heaven, not to do my own will, but the will of him who sent me" (John 6:29, 38).

These claims by Jesus led him into some direct clashes with the Jewish leaders, the political bosses of his day. Political bosses are not always right, but in many cases, if you want to win, they can deliver the votes. For Jesus, it was these very claims of his unity with God that brought a head-on clash with the Jewish leaders. On one occasion Jesus said to the Jewish leaders, "If God were your Father, you would love me, for I proceeded and came forth from God; I came not of my own accord, but he sent me" (John 8:42). He continued to direct some very pointed words to them.

The Jewish leaders became so enraged that they asked him, "Are we not right in saying you are a Samaritan and have a demon?" (John 8:48). They tried to pin the most vicious things they knew on him: being a Samaritan, those who were hated by the Jews, and being possessed of a demon, which meant he was associated with the devil. What they did was similar to reckless charges often made against others today in order to discredit them. Jesus denied the charges, but this illustrates the smear campaign that was waged against him.

The platform presented by Jesus to the Jewish leaders did not appear to be easy. The same was true of his platform to the people at large, although he generally did not denounce the general populace with the intensity that he did the Jewish leaders. In fact, the Pharisees and scribes criticized him for eating with ordinary people — the tax collectors and sinners. He looked on the crowds, not in a spirit of condemnation, but with compassion and pity. It was said of him, "When he saw the crowds, he had compassion on them, because they were harassed and helpless, like sheep without a shepherd" (Matthew 9:36). Before he fed the 4,000, he had compassion on the crowd. The ten lepers moved him to pity.

However, there were occasions when he spoke quite directly to the crowds in a manner that was not designed to get votes. On one occasion the crowds were increasing around him and he said that they were a part of an evil generation because the people did not have any real faith. Instead of faith, they were seeking a sign.

On another occasion the crowds pressed upon him when a man broke in to ask him to divide an inheritance, but Jesus used the occasion to tell a parable on stewardship. We are told of the time when great multitudes accompanied him. Apparently Jesus was becoming weary of the crowds following him because all it wanted was to see what it could get from him. He responded by three statements that seem designed to keep people away. His statements were harsh and he was not going to win votes in this way.

He said that those who followed him had to love him more than their own parents and family; that "whoever does not bear his own cross and come after me, cannot be my disciple" (Luke 14:27), and "whoever of you does not renounce all that he has cannot be my disciple" (Luke 14:33).

Jesus was committed to a cause greater than himself in which humankind's measure of victory was not his measure of victory.

A political campaign is a grueling affair, especially for presidential candidates. They must speak several times a day. They must meet their campaign managers for many conferences. Every time they come to a new city they must confer with local politicians. This is all necessary and we should not criticize it. It is a part of the governmental process and every citizen should take an interest in it.

We must not forget that Jesus' campaign was also something very grueling. It drained him of energy all the time. On Jesus' way to the house of Jairus to heal his daughter, the crowds pressed about him. Suddenly he felt energy go forth from his body. When he mentioned this, the disciples dismissed it as insignificant because of the crowds. Then he spotted the lady who had been sick for years and only wanted to touch the hem of his garment, which she did, and she was healed. Jesus set a grueling pace for himself.

His only relief came when he went off by himself to pray. He did this in times of sorrow, but he also did it regularly so he would gain strength for his campaign.

In all of this he was giving of himself for others. He said, "I must preach the good news of the kingdom of God" (Luke 4:43). This was nothing optional for him; he had to do it.

In the upper room before his death, the fourth gospel records that after Judas received the bread, he left Jesus and the other disciples. Jesus then said, "Now is the Son of man glorified, and in him God is glorified" (John 13:31). This was followed by the betrayal and the crucifixion. Jesus was here to glorify God; he was not here to gain votes. It looked as if the whistle-stop campaign was derailed on Calvary.

Victory came three days later with the empty tomb. It was a victory gained only for the minority, for those who through faith knew and saw the risen Christ and dedicated their lives to him as the supreme cause of their lives.

Chapter 4

Concerning The Nature And Destiny Of Humankind

If any man would come after me, let him deny himself and take up his cross and follow me. For whoever would save his life will lose it; and whoever loses his life for my sake and the gospel's will save it. For what does it profit a man, to gain the whole world and forfeit his life? — Mark 8:34-36

What meaning do we give to life? Is there any meaning? Or, is there any meaning to death? The two are closely related. These are questions that Jesus faced. What was life's purpose? Jesus found it on the cross. These are also questions we face. It is Jesus who gives us the answers.

Jesus had gone with his disciples to the village of Caesarea Philippi. When Jesus questioned him, Peter made his famous confession that Jesus was the Christ. Following this Jesus began to teach the disciples of his death which was to come. He told them he would be killed by the Jewish leaders. It was then that Peter began to rebuke Jesus and, as Matthew records the story, declared that such things should never happen to Jesus.

Jesus rebuked Peter, telling him that he was not looking at life from the viewpoint of God. Jesus then gathered the disciples and others around him and declared, "If any man would come after me, let him deny himself and take up his cross and follow me. For whoever would save his life will lose it; and whoever loses his life for my sake and the gospel's will save it. For what does it profit a man, to gain the whole world and forfeit his life?" (Mark 8:34-36).

These words are not merely good advice to be taken or ignored. They are the unbreakable truth. They are as true as if Jesus had said, "Day follows night." These ideas of Jesus are recorded six times in the gospels and the idea is expressed in each of the four gospels. The ideas incorporated in these words are so profound that it is evident that Jesus was speaking of the true nature and destiny of man.

When we consider the nature and destiny of man as discussed by Jesus, we see that the nature of man in the view of Jesus was that man, by himself, totally inadequate to meet and face life and find any meaning to life. We are told that Jesus knew what was in man. He knew because he was both human and divine. Furthermore, we know that he was tempted as we are, yet did not sin.

Jesus knew that humans are filled with pride, pride in their own ability to work out their own destinies, but they always fail. That is why he declared, "Blessed are the poor in spirit," blessed are those who know how inadequate they are, and turn to God for help (Matthew 5:3).

The gospels are filled with stories of those whom Jesus helped when they turned to him. Many came to him because they found themselves inadequate to meet their spiritual or physical needs. These include people such as the paralytic to whom Jesus said his sins were forgiven, the woman at the well, the demoniac boy, Zacchaeus, and many others.

The basic human sin is our attempt to "go it alone." Whenever we try to do so, we fail. This is one of the great lessons of the scriptures. It was the cause of the failure of the people who tried to build the tower of Babel. The book of Proverbs is filled with statements such as "A man's pride will bring him low, but he who is lowly in spirit will obtain honor" (Proverbs 29:23). Jesus declared, "Every one who exalts himself will be humbled, and he who humbles himself will be exalted" (Luke 14:11). Saint Paul said, "Let any one who thinks that he stands take heed lest he fall" (1 Corinthians 10:12). A modern expression of this idea is "Whom the gods would destroy, they first make drunk with power."

Jesus saw this tendency of pride in humans. To those who humble themselves to seek his help, he gave that help, and still gives it today.

Jesus set forth conditions by which he could help people. These conditions demand surrender of one's life to him. "Whoever would save his life will lose it; but whoever loses his life for my sake, he will save it" (Mark 8:35). When Jesus first asked the fishermen and others to follow him, they did not realize what was in store. From what they had already seen and heard, perhaps they felt that Jesus had charisma. He told them that if they were going to follow him, they must bear a cross even as he would bear a cross. The full meaning of this did not penetrate the minds of the disciples until the day of Jesus' death. Even then they believed he had failed and they had wasted their time.

Every great leader has demanded a cross of his followers. King Arthur insisted upon conditions before a man could become a Knight of the Round Table. Everyone had to swear to speak no slander, nor listen to it; to live lives of the purest chastity; to ride abroad helping make right the wrongs he saw; to honor his own word as if it were God's; to uphold Christ.

At the beginning of World War II, Winston Churchill promised the British no easy time. He said they would need blood, sweat, and tears to meet the challenge of 1940 and subsequent years. Likewise, Jesus said that the real challenge of life could only be met through the acceptance of a cross. He said that this was true of his own life. Jesus never tried to seek an easier way for himself than he demanded of his followers. The opposite is also true: He demands that his followers live by the same challenge and sacrifice that he himself showed. He added that whoever does not do this cannot be his disciple.

Jesus indicated that the cross was a part of his own destiny. He then called on his own disciples to share it with him. What Jesus was saying is universally true: that one who seeks first the security of his own life, the security of this world, ends by losing that which makes life truly significant: membership in the kingdom of God.

Earlier Jesus had declared that people do not live by bread alone. People live by the word of God, the truths of God. Humankind finds its true freedom and true meaning in these truths, not in seeking first the bread or the powers or the things of this world. Life only finds meaning and its true destiny when life is caught up in a larger meaning beyond the present. "Whoever loses his life for my sake and the gospel's will save it" (Mark 8:35).

While life often seems to confront people with many choices, there are basically only two choices, the road of self-interest and the road of self-denial. The road Christ suggests will find the fulfillment of our destiny is the road in which we bear our crosses, in which we serve unselfishly, "for my sake." Before each is the choice of the higher life which is the way of blessedness. One has the choice of the high road or the low road. The high road leads to one's true destiny, by surrender of life to Christ.

The principle of surrender is not confined to the initial phase of our conversion. To surrender our lives to Christ is a continuing principle to be followed throughout the converted life. As one faces problems, they can only find answers by surrendering them into God's hands. He shares and answers our problems when we listen to him. The answers are not always immediately apparent. However, to surrender life to Christ means a surrender of will and motive and every problem.

Jesus suggested that we might make very poor choices in life. When Emperor Charlemagne was buried, he was placed in a tomb, not as if sleeping, but seated on a throne in the robe of state, with an open Bible on his knee. One finger pointed to the words that spoke when he could no longer speak: "What does it profit a man if he gains the whole world and loses or forfeits his life?"

The soul is not something hidden away inside of us, to be saved by Sunday worship and labeled for heaven. The soul is life. What does it profit if a person gains a half million dollars in the bank and loses his or her health?

Jesus emphasized this idea when he called people to commit themselves to the cause of his kingdom. He declared that one must lose one's life, but it must be done for his sake. On one occasion he suggested that no one who put a hand to the plow and looked back was fit for the kingdom of heaven. Again, anyone who claims to be his follower must love him more than one's own family. Only by making such choices will one find the kingdom. Only in that way will one find life.

This is the law of the kingdom of God. One must have a loyalty and devotion beyond one's self. A biographer of Adolph Ochs, for many years the publisher of the *New York Times*, tells that Ochs liked money, but he liked something else more. Above all else he liked the idea of creating a truly great newspaper and he never allowed himself to be deflected from that goal by opportunities to make money outside of the newspaper business. The health of society needs men and women in business and the professions who are loyal to higher ideals than only to make money.

In the mid-1950s, a young man, Jack Theiss, went to Korea as a business manager of his denomination's mission. He expected to stay only a few years. In the aftermath of the Korean War, Theiss saw orphaned children. They were without parents, without food or shelter. Children were begging on the streets. Theiss was perturbed by the restlessness of these boys and began to visit their hangouts around Seoul. He talked to them as they cooked their stew from scraps found in garbage dumps. It was hard to gain rapport with the boys, for they trusted no one.

Out of his own meager salary, he began to feed and clothe the boys. He found housing for some. Eventually his denomination's mission board appropriated some money and set up a camp on the edge of the city. Some GIs helped by building two Quonset huts. The boys were taught how to plant vegetable gardens and a rice paddy. These efforts grew into a school and home called Angel Haven.

This principle holds for churches. No church can ever call itself truly Christian unless it has an outreach into all the world. Too often we find churches that are interested in a vague way in being a better church or a church that is growing in numbers. The question that must be asked is: What is the secret of a growing congregation? It is the congregation that has an ever-enlarging view and interest in contributing to the support of the mission program of the Christian church. Everything hinges on what a congregation gives to missions and outreach. An analysis of giving by individuals and families in the local church usually shows that the people who give most generously to the program of the local church are those who give most generously to missions. A congregation can build a fine physical plant and have a fine local program for its members, but such a congregation must remember that it is in danger of spending too much on itself and lose its own soul. What Jesus said of the danger to individuals also holds for congregations.

Something that should not be overlooked is the destiny of man in the final judgment. Jesus emphasized such a judgment when he declared that "whoever is ashamed of me and of my words, of him will the Son of man be ashamed when he comes in his glory and the glory of the Father" (Luke 9:26). Our destiny is not limited to losing our life here for Christ. Unless we lose our lives for him in this world, we shall never find ourselves in companionship with him after death. We are required to witness to his power and his words and his truths here or he will not recognize us after death. Man's destiny cannot be understood unless we find meaning after death as well as meaning in the causes to which we commit ourselves on this earth.

This is summarized in Jesus' parable of the judgment. In it he tells of his coming in glory. He associates himself with the needy and with the great causes of humanity. Those who fed the hungry, who clothed the naked, and who visited those in prison in his name did it to him as well. Some failed. In the judgment he was ashamed of those who failed. They were cast into outer darkness.

Our destiny in this world, and in the world after death, is found in the ethical demands we recognize and fulfill in the name of Christ. "For whoever would save his life will lose it; but whoever loses his life for my sake, and the gospel's will save it" (Mark 8:35).

Chapter 5

Concerning The Kingdom Of God

Thy kingdom come, thy will be done on earth as it is in heaven. — Matthew 6:10

In the history of the Christian faith we usually associate the city of Damascus, Syria, with the transformation and surrender of Paul as he journeyed to that city. Today Damascus is located in the heart of the Muslim world. When one walks through the city, one is aware that the Christian faith is a minority religion.

One of the great religious centers of the city is a mosque that was once the great church of St. John the Baptist. To enter the building, one's shoes must first be removed. On one side of the mosque, where there had been an entrance to the ancient church, one can still see words carved into the stone. While one is somewhat depressed that another faith has taken over what was once a great Christian church, one finds new hope and courage for the future of Christ's kingdom when one reads, "Thy kingdom, O Christ, is an everlasting kingdom!"

Jesus often spoke of the kingdom. In the gospel according to Matthew the phrase "kingdom of heaven" occurs 32 times, and the more personalized "kingdom of God" another four times. In most of these instances Jesus is the speaker. The idea is expressed as well in the other gospel accounts, especially in Mark and Luke.

The gospel of Mark is the most concise account of Jesus' life. It shows more movement than any of the other gospels. After the first chapter describes his temptations in the wilderness, we read that Jesus came into Galilee, preaching the gospel of God, saying, "The time is fulfilled, and the kingdom of God is at hand; repent, and believe the gospel" (Mark 1:15).

We often use the same phrase. With different wording we pray for and speak of the kingdom of God and the kingdom of heaven. In the prayer that Jesus taught his disciples we find the phrase, "Thy kingdom come."

It is this kingdom that Jesus commanded his disciples to proclaim. When he sent out the seventy, he commanded them to tell those whom they healed that the kingdom was near.

When we examine what Jesus said concerning the kingdom, he is saying that the kingdom of God is a spiritual kingdom. This was in contrast to the prevailing Jewish ideas of the kingdom which had been believed by the Hebrew people for many centuries. Most of the prophets had believed that the Lord would intervene in human affairs at some particular time as the judge of people. Amos spoke of the "Day of the Lord," a final hour of God's judgment. A psalmist declared, "Thy kingdom is an everlasting kingdom, and thy dominion endures throughout all generations" (Psalm 145:13). Since Israel was a buffer state in the midst of great empires, it was not strange that the "kingdom" for the Jews took on the idea of nationalism. They believed that God would establish his reign through the exaltation of Israel. The keeping of the law was the thing on which the coming of the kingdom depended and pious Jews believed that if the chosen people would keep only two sabbaths in perfect obedience, the kingdom would come.

When Jesus spoke of the kingdom, he declared that conversion was necessary to find the kingdom. Jesus told Nicodemus that unless he was born anew he would not see the kingdom of God. The spiritual emphasis on the kingdom is seen in the first beatitude where Jesus said that the poor in spirit, those who had complete dependence on God, would be blessed, and would obtain the kingdom.

He also pointed out that the kingdom was not dependent on one's body. In fact, he said that no part of one's body should prevent one from entering the kingdom of God, suggesting thereby that the use or abuse of our bodies is a spiritual matter.

In one of his parables Jesus suggested that the kingdom of God could be compared to a mustard seed which, when sown on the ground, is the smallest of all shrubs. He was pointing out that little, and often seemingly insignificant, things contribute to the kingdom.

When the kingdom of God is defined in spiritual terms, it is apparent that humility is one of the characteristics of those who find the kingdom. Jesus had told people they must repent because the kingdom was at hand. He said that only if one turned and became like a child would he enter the kingdom of heaven. He told the proud chief priests and elders in the temple in Jerusalem that the tax collectors and harlots would go into the kingdom of God before they did. Humility is a requisite to find God's kingdom.

When one studies the New Testament references to the kingdom, we find it is something not limited to one's personal experience. This was emphasized by Jesus as he explained the parable of the sower to his disciples, telling them that it was to them that had been given the secret of the kingdom of God. We find the kingdom, and experience it, in a social setting as well as in individuals.

Further, Jesus spoke of the kingdom of God in the context of ethics and righteousness. In the Lord's Prayer he petitioned that "Thy kingdom come, thy will be done on earth as it is in heaven." It must be remembered that the Lord's Prayer, as recorded in the Sermon on the Mount, is found in a sermon in which Jesus emphasized righteousness and ethical living.

It is inconsistent for anyone to pray for the kingdom to come and then close his eyes to unrighteousness in the local community or in the world. For this reason the Christian has a responsibility to be aware of conditions in the world, and study the causes of instability. In many cases even the Christian will feel helpless to do anything that can change the course of events. The Christian, however, can always pray. The Christian can work to be a reconciler by understanding issues and peoples and explaining these to others as the opportunity arises.

One of the familiar references to the kingdom is Jesus' statement, "Seek first the kingdom of God and his righteousness and all these things shall be yours as well" (Matthew 6:33). What did he mean by "all these things" that shall be ours if we first seek the kingdom of God? The statement can be found in chapter 6 of Matthew and chapter 12 of Luke. Immediately before making the statement, Jesus tells people not to be anxious about food and clothing and the material things of life. He reminds them that God cares for all his creatures and that all of our anxieties about these things will not add one moment to life. He points out that the heavenly Father knows we need all these things and that we should trust him. With that background he warns against covetousness, declaring, "Seek first the kingdom of God."

Jesus emphasized that the kingdom of God was available to all people. However, any person who had experienced the kingdom has a responsibility to help others know it. His last command to his disciples was that they must be his witnesses in Jerusalem, Judea, Samaria, and to the ends of the earth.

Someone once asked Jesus if only a few would be saved. He advised that they seek to enter by the narrow door. Then, as he answered his questioners, he said that people would begin to knock and want to enter, claiming that they had once eaten and drunk with him. However, he called such people workers of iniquity because of their sins and that they would be thrust out of the kingdom of God. Then, he added, "Men will come from east and west, and from north and south, and sit at table in the kingdom of God. And ... some are last who will be first, and some are first who will be last" (Luke 13:29-30).

Thus we see that Jesus was condemning those who refused to bear their responsibilities in telling others of the kingdom. Matthew records that Jesus told the Pharisees that because the Jews had not proclaimed God's universal love and mercy as they should that "the kingdom of God will be taken away from you and given to a nation producing the fruits of it" (Matthew 21:43).

One of the paradoxes of the Christian faith is that the kingdom of God is something that is here but also something that is coming. The kingdom is not in the past; we do not look upon it as something present in the good old days. Jesus said, "No one who puts his hand to the plow and looks back is fit for the kingdom of God" (Luke 9:62).

The kingdom of God is the focal point for a life filled with the presence of Christ. When Jesus was at Bethsaida, he was followed by crowds. Jesus "welcomed them and spoke to them of the kingdom of God, and cured those who had need of healing" (Luke 9:11). This again illustrates that Jesus ministered to the whole person, the body as well as the spirit. People in that day experienced the kingdom of God when Jesus cured their bodies. It was something for the present life.

There is the story of a Russian youth who had become a conscientious objector to war through the reading of Tolstoy and the New Testament. He was brought before a magistrate. With strength of conviction, he told the judge of the life which loves its enemies, which does good to those who despitefully treat one, which overcomes evil with good, and which refuses to condone war.

"Yes," said the judge, "I understand. But you must be realistic. These laws you are talking about are the laws of the kingdom of God, and it has not yet come."

The young man straightened, and said, "Sir, I recognize that it has not come for you, nor yet for Russia or the world. But the kingdom of God has come for me. I cannot go on hating and killing as though it has not come." He was sentenced to prison for his position.

Every person must ask himself if he has experienced the kingdom of God.

Chapter 6

Concerning The Church

I tell you, you are Peter, and on this rock I will build my church, and the powers of death shall not prevail against it. — Matthew 16:18

As Jesus continued his campaign, he spoke on various subjects. One of these was the church, although surprisingly he said very little about it. However, what he did say about the church was so profound that even today we cannot understand fully the importance of his remarks.

Jesus had been in Galilee. He left that region and, with his disciples, went north along the Jordan River. About fifteen miles north of the Sea of Galilee, east of the Jordan River, is Mount Hermon, which many biblical scholars believe to be the Mount of Transfiguration. Nestled at the south end of Mount Hermon is the small village of Caesarea Philippi. It was to this area that Jesus took his disciples.

It was here that Jesus asked the disciples, "Who do you say that the Son of Man is?" Some answered that he was John the Baptist, others that he was Elijah or Jeremiah or one of the prophets. Then he pressed them for their own ideas, asking, "But who do you say that I am?" Peter replied, "You are the Christ, the Son of the living God." Jesus replied that this was something that had been revealed to Peter by God, declaring, "I tell you, you are Peter, and on this rock I will build my church, and the powers of death shall not prevail against it" (Matthew 16:13-19).

When we consider Christ's teaching about the church, we must always remember that it is Christ's church. It is not humankind's church. Too often people talk about the church as they talk about some other organization in society.

People equate the church with a service club, a lodge, a farm organization, all on an equal basis. Such a comparison cannot be made. The church is unique when it is compared with any other organization in the community. It is unique because God and Christ are unique. Christ said, "I will build my church." This, we must never forget.

On his way to Greece in Caesar's campaign against Pompey, the fleet was buffeted by a terrible storm. Caesar tried to calm the fears of the sailors with the words, "Remember, you carry Caesar and his fortunes." That was a rash remark. In the case of Christ, it is true. The church carries Christ and his redeeming fortunes and no storm can overwhelm it.

The whole church of Christ was present one night in a little ship tossed by the sea: Peter, James, John, Matthew, Bartholomew, and the rest of the disciples. If the ship had gone down, the entire church of Christ would have been lost, for these were the men chosen to found it. But the ship did not go down. It did not sink, for Christ was with it. Through the years the church has not gone down, because Christ is with it.

Because it is Christ's church, it is a sin to tear it apart. This does not mean that by one grand decree all denominations should be united. It means that each one should recognize that Christians of all persuasions have a unity in Christ that should not be destroyed by bickering, fighting, and backbiting. This applies to local congregations, as well as for denominations.

There is a revealing incident that took place at the crucifixion of Jesus. According to custom the Roman soldiers could appropriate to themselves the garment of the victim. When they came to Jesus' coat, they discovered that it was seamless. If it was cut into four parts, one for each soldier, it would be ruined. For that reason they decided to keep it intact, and to cast lots for it. By so doing, according to the fourth gospel, the soldiers fulfilled the statement of the messianic Psalm, "They parted my garments among them, and for my clothing they cast lots" (Psalm 22:18; John 19:24).

The great preacher, Henry Ward Beecher, once used this idea in a prayer to express the desire for the unity of the church. He prayed that the church might be once again like the seamless robe of the Lord. This is a very appropriate comparison. The strife of the groups in the church, and the wrangling of factions, have tended to tear into pieces the sacred garment of the truth. The crucified one looks sadly on the miserable conflict that takes place in his name.

The message of the church is always the message of Christ, the one Christ who cannot be divided, because it is his church and his church cannot be divided any more than Christ himself can.

The statement of Christ to Peter at Caesarea Philippi shows that Jesus was building his church on ordinary people. He was referring to Peter as a person, but more than that, he was using Peter as a representative of the type of person on whom the church was to be built.

The small band of disciples were ordinary people, in some cases people who had little status in society. Several were fishermen. Some were despised tax collectors. Only one was from a so-called respectable society. His name was Judas, the only one who came from near Jerusalem.

This has always been evident in the history of the church. The church is not built by politicians. It is said that when people are elected to congress they seldom, if ever, join a church in Washington. There seems to be an unwritten rule that if they join a church in the capital, word of their doing so will reach the home folks who will interpret it to mean that the congressman is planning to stay in Washington for a long time. The folks back home will take care of that at the next election.

Paul expressed this idea as well. The church depends on ordinary people. To the Corinthians he wrote, "For consider your call, brethren; not many of you were wise according to worldly standards, not many were powerful, not many were of noble birth; but God chose what is foolish in the world to shame the wise, God chose what is weak in the world to shame the strong" (1 Corinthians 1:26-27). He refers to the Christians who were servants in the household of Caesar.

Not only has the church relied on ordinary people. It has also been very cosmopolitan. When Paul preached to the sophisticates in Athens, we are told that one who believed was Dionysius the Areopagite, a member of the leading group of citizens in the city. Another was Damaris, presumably a woman of the street. It was on a variety of people like these that Christ built his church.

Christ was building his church, then and now, by using ordinary people with various abilities, all of whom were necessary and all of whom could make a contribution to the church. "Some should be apostles, some prophets, some evangelists, some pastors and teachers ... for building up the body of Christ" (Ephesians 4:11-12).

In writing to the Corinthians, Paul compares the members of the church to the parts of the body, each of whom had a contribution to make to the total life of the church, declaring, "You are the body of Christ and individually members of it" (1 Corinthians 12:27). God appointed in the church helpers, administrators, speakers, prophets, teachers, said Paul. Each committed Christian has a part in the life and work of the church. Christ is building his church on the work of every Christian. Christ did not look to one apostle to do the work of the church; Christ does not look exclusively to the pastor to do the work of the church. The burdens of the church rest on every Christian. Any person who says, "He is the Christ, the Son of the living God," automatically finds responsibilities in the church.

Just because a group of people meets regularly for worship does not mean it is a community or a fellowship. It is essential that the fellowship be made real as each Christian accepts responsibility for mutual service and by breaking down the barriers that often divide people. This is the work of ordinary people, the Peters from the time the first apostles left their fishing nets to follow Jesus.

Several years ago, an ex-teacher over eighty years of age was found to have cancer. Her only son lived 1,000 miles away. The woman did not want to stay in the hospital. Active in her church, the members of that congregation rallied to help. The women of the congregation organized so that there was someone with the ill woman 24 hours a day — not for one week, not for a month, but for four months, until she died. This was the church at work.

Finally, we must remember that the church is eternal. "The powers of death" or the "gates of hell" shall not prevail against it (Matthew 16:18).

It is significant that while there was a systematic effort to destroy the church in communist Russia for three generations, the church survived and the efforts of a materialistic philosophy could not prevail against it. Perhaps a more serious threat to the church is the indifference of its members, the lack of zeal and dedication on the part of those on whom the church must depend for its effectiveness and witness.

The church is eternal because it is God's and God is eternal. Because God rules in this world and the eternities, the church cannot be destroyed. The powers of death shall not be victorious over it. When Hitler boasted that the German Reich would last 1,000 years, Martin Niemoller said, "To be optimistic, it may last 2,000 years, but it will not last eternally."

There is a story of a man who dreamed that he was in a city where there were many splendid and notable buildings — granite buildings that held the temples of finance, the great buildings of the universities, great theaters, and fine homes. In the midst of these buildings there stood a plain structure, humble and modest in comparison with the mighty buildings that looked down upon it. Men and women were going into and coming out of that humble structure.

One hundred years passed in the dream, and the man found himself again in the same city, but he could hardly recognize it, for all the great buildings upon which he had looked 100 years before had disappeared and other more imposing structures had taken their places. Still, in the midst of those great buildings stood the modest frame building, with men and women going in and out, just as he had seen them do a century earlier.

One thousand years passed, and the man returned to that same city, and again he noted a complete transformation. All buildings that he had seen before had vanished and new buildings with new architecture and new grandeur had taken their places — all except the little frame building, and out of it he saw men and women coming with the light of joy and satisfaction upon their faces. At length he asked some of the citizens what that building might be, and what was the explanation of its remaining unchanged and still frequented after all other buildings had vanished and disappeared. Then he learned the secret of the endurance of that one building: It was the house of God where people found the way of life eternal.

The ordinary people who make the confession of Peter that Jesus is the Christ qualify themselves for the task of helping Christ's church, which shall last through the eternities in spite of all adversities.

Chapter 7

Concerning The Unity Of Christians

> *I do not pray for these only, but also for those who are to believe in me through their word, that they may all be one; even as thou, Father, art in me, and I in thee, that they also may be in us, so that the world may believe that thou hast sent me.* — John 17:20-21

In chapter 17 of the gospel of John we find what is known as the high priestly prayer of Jesus. The scene is the upper room on the night of his betrayal. Jesus had just shared the Lord's Supper with his disciples. He then gave them instructions as recorded in chapters 14-16 of the fourth gospel. These are followed by the profound prayer of chapter 17.

The first portion of this prayer was for himself as he faced the cross. Then he prayed for his disciples and for God's power to keep them true to the faith. Beginning with verse 20 his prayer takes a sweep into the ageless future, and he prays for those in distant lands and for those through all the ages who will enter the Christian faith.

He declares, "I do not pray for these only (meaning the disciples), but also for those who are to believe in me through their word, that they may all be one; even as thou, Father, art in me, and I in thee, that they also may be in us, so that the world may believe that thou hast sent me" (John 17:20-21). Christ was not praying only for those who had followed him while he was on earth. His prayer was inclusive, to encompass all people throughout the ages.

This was a prayer for the church of which he is the head. His prayer was that all its members would be one as he and his Father are one. It was a part of his platform that there would be a unity among his followers through the ages. What was the unity for which he prayed?

It was not a unity of administration or organization. It was not an ecclesiastical unity. It was a unity of witness. Any reading of the scriptures shows that the relationship between Jesus and God was a union of love and obedience. Jesus is praying for a unity of love among those who claim his name, in which we love each other because we love him.

Christians will never organize all their churches in the same manner. Nor will all Christians worship God in the same way. There is, however, a body of doctrines, based on the scriptures, that finds a unity among Christians of many divergent traditions. The doctrinal statements of Eastern Orthodox, Protestants, and Roman Catholics indicate that all believe in what is known as the virgin birth, the necessity of Christ to die for the salvation of the world, his resurrection and his return.

Many people become confused because these beliefs are often expressed in different ways. Some traditions express these doctrines in a formal manner with a strict ceremonial approach; others are very informal. Some years after Jesus' ascension, Paul faced this problem a generation later when he wrote to Titus and advised, "Teach what befits sound doctrine" (Titus 2:1).

When these beliefs are expressed in different ways, people are sometimes confused. These differences should not be viewed in a negative way, because people are not robots. Jesus realized that the addition of more followers would mean a greater diversity of temperaments, backgrounds, and interests. Foreseeing this, he prayed that these outward differences would not keep the Holy Spirit from unifying their commitment to him.

Paul experienced the disunity of the church in Corinth. The Corinthians could squabble over anything. Factions were rampant. Some claimed to belong to Paul, Apollos, Cephas, or Christ (1 Corinthians 1:12-13). Paul urged the members of the church to make Christ their common loyalty, even if there were different ways to express that loyalty. "There are varieties of gifts, but the same spirit; and there are varieties of service, but the same Lord; and there are varieties of working, but it is the same God who inspires them all in everyone" (1 Corinthians 12:4). Unfortunately, such words are sometimes ignored by those who refuse to recognize that Christ is available to all.

This danger that often divides Christians finds an Old Testament precedent among the people of God in ancient Israel. When the land was divided by Joshua, the half tribe of Manasseh, the tribe of Reuben, and the tribe of Gad were given land east of the Jordan River, in the land of Gilead. As they crossed the Jordan, they built an altar of great size. When word of this reached the other tribes, there was such turmoil that they mobilized for war against the two and one-half tribes.

Fortunately, there were some who thought they should investigate the situation before they engaged in a fratricidal war. Men from the tribes west of the Jordan went to the two and one-half eastern tribes to inquire the reason for the altar, accusing them of treachery in building the altar and thus rebelling against God.

The leaders of the two and one-half tribes denied any rebellion against God or against the tribes west of the Jordan. They said they had built the altar "to be a witness between us and you, and between the generations after us, that we do perform the service of the Lord ... Behold the copy of the altar of the Lord, which our fathers made, not for burnt offerings, nor for sacrifice, but to be a witness between us and you" (Joshua 22:27-28).

Too often there are church groups that fail to see that others are witnessing to Christ, though they take a different approach.

Jesus was expressing his desire for a vital unity among all who would follow him in the future. A short time before he had declared that he was the true vine. He said, "I am the vine and you are the branches. He who abides in me, and I in him, he it is that bears much fruit, for apart from me you can do nothing. If a man does not abide in me, he is cast forth as a branch and withers" (John 15:5-6). All the branches, large and small, are vital if the church is to grow and bear fruit.

The purpose of Jesus' prayer included more than a reference to the disciples. It was a prayer for those who would believe through the ensuing ages. It was a prayer "so that the world may believe that thou hast sent me" (John 17:21). This was a prayer for the universal church.

It was a prelude to the last words of Jesus as recorded in the gospel of Matthew: "All authority in heaven and on earth has been given to me. Go thereforth and make disciples of all nations, baptizing them in the name of the Father and of the Son and of the

Holy Spirit, teaching them to observe all that I have commanded you; and lo, I am with you always, to the close of the age" (Matthew 28:18-20).

This prayer was for the missionary outreach of the church. When one reads this prayer as well as other teachings of Jesus concerning the outreach of the gospel, one finds evidence that no congregation is truly following Christ if it is not mission-minded.

This is illustrated by a congregation that was active in supporting missions. Its own facilities were inadequate for its program. This resulted in its constructing new facilities in 1967. In 1989, the congregation celebrated the burning of the note that represented the money it had borrowed. That congregation could have paid its debt ten years earlier, but it did not want to decrease its mission giving, even to become debt-free.

Christians of the United States probably have given more money for missions than the people of any other country in the world. Missionaries have been sent to many other countries. While all of the missionaries have gone out in the name of Christ, it is ironic that some of the supporting churches in the United States have encouraged their missionaries to have nothing to do with others who have different approaches. Such attitudes are in defiance of Jesus' prayer "that they may all be one" (John 17:21).

When World War II began, missionaries of many European churches were cut off from their home support as their countries were engaged in war efforts or were under foreign domination. It was then that churches in the United States began to help missionaries from the European churches. With the slogan, "Let there be no over-looking and no over-lapping," the European missionaries were supported by the generosity of American churches for several years. This illustrates the fulfillment of Jesus' prayer, "that they may all be one."

Jesus' prayer in the upper room was a universal prayer. It was an inclusive prayer. It was in effect a prayer for Christians of all backgrounds to work together in a cooperative spirit. Jesus was praying for the unity of Christians in their beliefs, their commitment to make the gospel known, in their prayers together, in the wise use of their resources, in their mutual efforts to make Christ known.

Chapter 8

Concerning Prayer

He told them ... they ought always to pray and not lose heart. — Luke 18:1

The area of Christian living where most people feel inadequate is prayer. While we realize the necessity of prayer, this feeling is intensified when we read that Jesus told his disciples "they ought always to pray and not lose heart."

Often we say that we are too busy to pray. Yet, that is the main reason we should pray. It was Martin Luther who spoke on the subject of having time for prayer: "I have so much to do today that I must spend several hours in prayer."

Jesus emphasized the necessity of prayer. He lived it. When the disciples saw him pray they realized that they, in comparison, were lacking something in their own lives. After their request that he teach them to pray, he gave them a pattern for prayer which we know as the Lord's Prayer. In the gospel account given Luke, the disciples asked Jesus to teach them to pray. In the Sermon on the Mount the prayer is the same, although there is no record that Jesus had been asked about prayer by the disciples.

The gospel accounts indicate that Jesus often spoke of prayer. He sometimes spoke directly about it; other times he told parables concerning prayer. In the context of the platform of Jesus, it is necessary for us to examine some of the things that Jesus said concerning prayer. Jesus said so much about prayer that it would take many books to touch all of the facets of prayer mentioned by Jesus.

Jesus looked upon prayer as something that was natural. The fact that the disciples asked him to show them how to pray indicates how natural it was for Jesus to pray.

We gain insight on this subject when we turn to the only account of the early life of Jesus, recorded in the second chapter of Luke. It includes the story of Jesus who remained in the temple in Jerusalem when his parents had left to go home to Nazareth. The story indicates that his parents went to Jerusalem every year "as their custom was," and this can be validly interpreted to mean that Jesus had been there previously. All of the characteristics of a religious and devout person were a part of his life — worship, prayer, helping others, a stewardship of life. His consistency of prayer is found in the numerous times he left the disciples to find a quiet place to stay.

Jesus prayed to seek the will of God in his life. In the Lord's Prayer, Jesus used the phrase, "Thy will be done on earth as it is in heaven" (Matthew 6:10). Later, in the Garden of Gethsemane, Jesus prayed as he faced the cross, "Not my will but Thine be done" (Luke 22:42).

In these two statements of Jesus we have the clash between the human will and the divine will. In the days preceding Calvary it was apparent that Jesus' work would end in failure, that evil would overwhelm him. There is always a clash between the human will and God's will. There are times that the human will seems to offer the brightest picture. At times the will of God seems to be the blackest.

Dr. George Buttrick has pointed out that the real conflict in the world is not between the cause of one nation and that of another nation, not between rival ideologies in the world, not between communism and capitalism. The real conflict is between the will of man and the will of God. The fourth gospel tells that Jesus with his disciples crossed the brook Kidron where there was a garden. That was the Garden of Gethsemane where Jesus agonized over his destiny. The brook Kidron is the great divide of history. It is in such circumstances that every conflict takes place, the eternal conflict between the will of God and the will of man.

When Jesus spoke concerning prayer, one of his emphases was that in prayer we seek truly to do God's will. This may mean persecution, unpopularity, or being crucified, as it did for Jesus.

Jesus also speaks concerning the need for prayer in the crises of life. Prayer can help overcome temptation. In the accounts of the temptations of Jesus, we are told that Jesus was led by the Holy Spirit. This is part of the life of prayer, for it must always be accompanied by the power of the Holy Spirit. We are told by Luke that after his experience in the wilderness, "Jesus returned in the power of the Spirit into Galilee" (Luke 4:14). In the crisis caused by the temptations, it is evident that he was victorious through prayer.

Prayer can aid in times of sorrow. In chapter 14 of Matthew, we find Jesus facing the crisis of sorrow as he learned of the death of John the Baptist at the hands of Herod. This was a severe blow to Jesus. John had been the one who had pointed to Jesus as the Savior of the world. John was responsible for focusing the attention of the people on Jesus. Then, too, John and Jesus were cousins. Because of this kinship, Jesus was moved to great sorrow. When Jesus heard of the fate of John, he went off by himself to pray.

However, when the crowds heard he was in the vicinity, many people came to him. It was a great throng. Jesus, in spite of his sorrow, had compassion on them, and healed their sick. This was followed by the feeding of the 5,000. In spite of his sorrow, he did not let the people in need shift for themselves. After feeding the 5,000, he dismissed the crowds and told the disciples to cross the lake by themselves. He then "went up into the hills by himself to pray" (Matthew 14:23). He served the people but at the same time prayer was his way of meeting the crisis brought by sorrow.

Prayer can also fortify us for difficult times. In chapter 17 of the fourth gospel, Jesus was in the upper room before he went out to meet those who would put him on trial and eventually kill him. After speaking to his disciples, "He lifted up his eyes to heaven and said, 'Father, the hour has come; glorify thy Son that the Son may glorify thee' " (John 17:1). He fortified himself for the impending crisis with prayer.

Further, we see that Jesus emphasized prayer for others as well as for himself. In the upper room Jesus said he was not praying only for himself, but for the disciples: "I am praying for them; I am not praying for the world but for those whom thou hast given me, for they are thine" (John 17:9). Jesus had a concern for the mission of the disciples, as he also said that "I do not pray for these only, but also for those who are to believe in me through their word" (John 17:20). His prayer was for the ongoing movement of the church through the ages to come.

Earlier Jesus had spoken in a similar manner. He saw the great crowds of people in need, harassed and helpless, like sheep without a shepherd. He then pointed out that the needs of the world for spiritual leadership were great. "The harvest is plentiful but the laborers are few." He commanded, "Pray therefore the Lord of the harvest to send out laborers into his harvest" (Matthew 9:38).

Jesus was concerned that the message he represented and embodied should be proclaimed to all. Dedicated and consecrated people were needed. Jesus was very concerned with ministerial supply. Studies by several denominations indicate that in the twenty-first century, there will be a shortage of pastors for local congregations. Jesus suggested that we must pray for that need to be fulfilled.

Jesus further suggested that prayer must fulfill the desires of the human soul. Prayer must not be done for outward appearances. Referring to one of the common practices of some of the Jewish leaders, Jesus told his followers that when they prayed they should not be like the hypocrites who loved to stand and pray in the synagogue and at the street corners so that they could be seen by men. Rather than do that, said Jesus, one should go into his room and shut the door and pray to the Father in secret, for he will hear whenever a sincere prayer is offered to him.

Prayer shows the deep desires of one's soul and an abiding faith. This was expressed by Jesus when he told the disciples that whatever they asked in prayer, if they believed, they would receive it. All prayer must be lifted to God "in Jesus' name." This is the criterion for the Christian's prayer. It is especially important to pray in Jesus' name when we ask for things.

Some years ago a woman asked a famous pastor if it was acceptable to pray for a new fur coat. The pastor's reply, "Yes, if you pray for it in Jesus' name." There is a great deal of difference between asking God for a new fur coat and asking God for a new fur coat "in Jesus' name." When one asks God for something for himself or herself "in Jesus' name," one is forced to consider the hungry of the world, the refugees and homeless, the needs for church programs, and all one's obligations to God.

Finally, we can always depend on God when we come to him in prayer. Paul emphasized this truth when he declared that "God is faithful" (1 Corinthians 1:9). He is faithful in listening to our prayers. Prayer is a part of faith. If no faith was present, it would not only be useless, but foolish, to pray, for Jesus said, "Whatever you ask in prayer, you will receive, if you have faith" (Matthew 21:22).

If we pray in the spirit of Christ, we will receive from God the things that meet our need and are consistent with his will, and which will fulfill his desires for the fullest development of our lives. Humans sometimes will be disappointed because they feel God is not listening. As a good parent does not give his child everything the child might desire, so God only gives us the things that are consistent with our best interests. While disappointments come and we do not always see the will of God clearly, we believe that what Jesus said about prayer is important. The command still comes to us today as it came to the disciples that we must "always pray and not lose heart" (Luke 18:1).

Chapter 9

Concerning Forgiveness

> *And forgive us our debts, as we also have forgiven our debtors ... For if you forgive men their trespasses, your heavenly Father will also forgive you; but if you do not forgive men their trespasses, neither will your Father forgive your trespasses.* — Matthew 6:12-14

John Wesley, the founder of the movement that became the Methodist church, hardly ever preached without describing the lost state of human beings. The first part of his sermon was usually a description of a coming judgment on the sins of mankind. He tells in his journal of an experience he had in the English town of Bath. "I preached at Bath. Some of the rich and great were present, to whom, as the rest, I declared with all plainness of speech: 1. that by nature they were all children of wrath; 2. that all their natural tempers were corrupt and abominable; 3. all their words and works — which could never be any better but by faith; and that, 4. a natural man has no more faith than a devil, if so much. One of them, my Lord, stayed patiently until I came to the middle of the fourth head; then starting up, he said, "Tis hot! 'Tis very hot' and ran down stairs as fast as he could."

The great preacher, John Henry Jowett, commenting on this entry of Wesley, said that Lord should have stayed until Wesley got to the heart of the text: "The Son of Man is come to seek and to save that which was lost" (Luke 19:10). Then he would have learned that over against the blackness of judgment there is the shining light of forgiveness. It is one of the great accomplishments of the gospel that it holds these two seeming opposites together in a divine unity. If we are strictly judged, we know also the experience of a divine forgiveness.

Both the idea of forgiveness and the need of forgiveness stand out in the entire Bible. In the Old Testament the blood of goats and other rituals were used to take care of guilt. In the New Testament the need of forgiveness is emphasized by Jesus, but the entire approach to the problem is changed from the Old Testament where it was man's merit that earned forgiveness to the New Testament idea that the initiative in bringing about forgiveness was taken by God.

Jesus often spoke of sin, failure, forgiveness, and reconciliation. Because of this it is necessary to examine carefully some of the things Jesus said on these subjects as they are related to the forgiveness of injuries.

The thought of forgiveness assumes our failure. A sense of failure is necessary on our part if one is to be forgiven. No one should draw into his own little shell, assuming that he does not fail. Paul declared, "All have sinned and fallen short of the glory of God" (Romans 3:23). The writer of 1 John said, "If we say we have no sin, we deceive ourselves, and the truth is not in us" (1 John 1:8).

There are those who will look at their neighbors and then claim that they, themselves, are free from a particular fault. The story is told of a gray-haired lady, long a member of her community and church. As she departed from church one Sunday morning, she said to the pastor, "That was a wonderful sermon, just wonderful. Everything you said applies to someone I know."

Jesus once told of the Pharisee who thanked God that he was not like other men. That Pharisee thought he was free from the sins which he condemned, although he had many sins for which he should repent — pride, arrogance, snobbery, self-righteousness, and contempt. It is possible to condemn sins of which we are not guilty while remaining complacent toward those of which we are guilty. This is the normal way to avoid condemning ourselves. One can easily feel so virtuous and so pleased with oneself because one's abhorrence of sins that one does not commit makes the sins one does commit pass unnoticed. For this reason no man is qualified to pass moral judgment on his neighbor; everyone has sins of his own that make such judgment presumptuous. Jesus condemned such thinking by asking, "Why do you see the speck that is in your brother's eye, but do not notice the log that is in your own eye? First, take the log out of your own eye, and then you will see clearly to take the speck out of your brother's eye" (Luke 6:41-42).

In reading the scriptures, we see that Jesus had a larger idea of failure than that which the people of his day and many contemporary people have. In the Sermon on the Mount Jesus condemned not just the person who killed another, but he also said that anyone who is angry with his brother is liable to judgment. Also, lustful thoughts are as sinful as adultery. The idea of an eye for an eye and a tooth for a tooth was enlarged by Jesus when he equated failing God when we showed hatred for someone. Time and again Jesus expressed the idea that we can fail God by motive and thought as well as overt act. When we realize this, we know we have sinned. Sin means that repentance is necessary; it means forgiveness is necessary if we are to be reconciled to God and our neighbor.

Also, Jesus set forth certain conditions that we must meet if we are to be forgiven. He declared, "Judge not, and you will not be judged; condemn not, and you will not be condemned; forgive, and you will be forgiven; give, and it will be given to you, good measure, pressed down, shaken together, running over, will be put into your lap. For the measure you give will be the measure you get back" (Luke 6:37-38). Notice the combination package of virtues he mentions: humility by not judging, forgiving, giving. These are all related.

Christ confronts us with a definite alternative: either you will pardon, or you cannot be pardoned; either you will know the joy and peace of forgiveness or you will build an insurmountable barrier between God's grace and yourself.

Jesus also emphasized these conditions in the Lord's Prayer: "For if you forgive men their trespasses, your heavenly Father also will forgive you" (Matthew 6:14). If we fail God in our relations with our fellow men, we will not receive God's forgiveness.

Among the conditions of forgiveness is that we must continually be forgiving. "Whenever" said Jesus, "you stand praying, forgive, if you have anything against anyone; so that your Father also who is in heaven may forgive your trespasses" (Mark 11:25).

On another occasion Peter came to Jesus and asked, "Lord, how often shall my brother sin against me, and I forgive him? As many as seven times?" Jesus answered him, "I do not say to you seven times, but seventy times seven" (Matthew 18:21-22). While

Jesus had a larger idea of failure than most people, he also had a much larger idea of forgiveness.

In all of these conditions, one thing stands out: The prime consideration for our own forgiveness is that we forgive all who injure us, and pray for them.

Lastly, forgiveness is necessary for a reconciliation between people and God and two people.

In society an offender must "prove" himself for a certain length of time after committing an offense against society.

Years ago, a man who had been released from the state prison came to the polling precinct of a municipality to vote in the September primary election. Because nothing was known of the condition of his release, he was allowed to vote. Before the general election in November, one of the elected officials checked with the state parole board and found that the man had been paroled but not pardoned. Because he was not in full standing as a citizen, when he came to vote in November, he was denied that privilege.

Any time that an offender is treated in a way that will encourage the repetition of the offense, it is an offense to God and a disservice to society and to the offender. However, for the Christian, the real intent of forgiveness is the moral and spiritual rehabilitation of the offender, his reconciliation to God. It is not just parole, but full pardon. The Christian view of forgiveness does not wait for the offender to repent.

This is the love of God described by Paul: "God shows his love for us in that while we were yet sinners Christ died for us" (Romans 5:8). This is the love that tries to bring the offender to repentance. This is not done by vindictive methods, but methods of good will — to love your enemies and do good to those who hate you, bless those who curse you and pray for those who abuse you, and, in that way, you will be sons of the most high.

Several years ago, several people were arrested for protesting the launching of nuclear submarines at New Haven, Connecticut. A news dispatch told that the sheriff who was custodian of the pacifists who were in the New Haven jail complained that they were talking with other inmates. The prisoners who had been arrested for protesting were showing such love and good spirits to the other prisoners that the sheriff did not know what to do with them. He was quoted as saying, "They've got to stop preaching non-violent resistance to the other prisoners. Some of the inmates are getting stirred up. This isn't India. We aren't staffed to cope with that sort of thing." Their witness was in the tradition of Paul who loved his jailers so much that the whole praetorian guard came to know that his imprisonment was because of his commitment to Christ. Obviously, these protestors held nothing but good will and love for the jailers. The sheriff could not understand Christian love sufficiently to cope with it.

Forgiveness is not merely acquittal. It is re-creation. It is a new alliance with God that calls for a new alliance with others. We must remember that there is no easy pardon. One who pardons easily does not pardon at all. Pardon is not only forgetting. A noble mother does not merely forget the shame of her wayward son. She remembers it, yet forgives, in the daily grief of her soul. When Jesus was washing the feet of Judas before the betrayal, Jesus had already forgiven him — while we were yet sinners. Jesus grieved, suffered, died, and thus forgave.

We must keep praying the prayer, "Forgive us our trespasses." Only God can forgive sins and only he by his love can forgive our sins. Only he can quicken in us the forgiving spirit.

Visitors to castles in Europe are often shown hidden doors leading to secret passages, and are told: This is how help came when the castle was held in a siege that could not be broken. Humankind is a prisoner to a helpless will that is filled with sin. But there is a secret way. Anyone can have contact with a vast country beyond one's own self, besieged by sin, for a person can pray, "Forgive us our trespasses, as we forgive those who trespass against us." Then, as a forgiven person, one can say to a brother or sister, "I forgive you, as I trust you to forgive me." In that way the siege is lifted.

"Be kind to one another, tenderhearted, forgiving one another, even as God for Christ's sake has forgiven you" (Ephesians 4:32).

Chapter 10

Concerning Possessions And Money Matters

No one can serve two masters; for either he will hate the one and love the other, or will be devoted to the one and despise the other. You cannot serve God and mammon. — Matthew 6:24

During a political campaign, we often feel that we have heard the last word on some subjects. Often we wish it were the last word! Sometimes candidates speak so often on one subject that they seem to "turn people off."

In a like manner, Jesus might be accused of being a Johnny One Note. When one looks at the gospels, the one subject on which he spoke more than any other was our relationship to our possessions and money. As he conducted his campaign, we find that more than 30% of his recorded discourses deal with possessions and money matters.

If pastors are to preach a full gospel, they must preach on money. If they do not, they are not true to the Bible. They are guilty of giving people a false sense of security by not pointing out that what they give to the church, their attitudes toward money, how they earn their money, and how they spend their money are all involved in their ultimate destiny.

Jesus dealt with our attitudes toward money and possessions more than he did with the subjects of faith, prayer, death, and eternal life. Of course, eternal life and our possessions are very closely related, and people who do not have the right attitude toward their possessions in this life would not find themselves comfortable with God after death.

Our use of money and material possessions is essentially a spiritual matter. What each gives to the church of Jesus Christ is one of the real measures of spirituality. One cannot avoid this by saying that others do not give or that in another church the people do not give as much. Jesus emphasized on many occasions that each person will be held accountable for his stewardship.

One of Jesus' early statements, part of the Sermon on the Mount, reads, "No one can serve two masters; for either he will hate the one and love the other, or he will be devoted to the one and despise the other. You cannot serve God and mammon" (Matthew 6:24).

This statement of Jesus is not a threat. Rather, it is a comment on life in a parable that speaks to one of the great truths of life. A master in that day had life and death control over the servant. Knowing this, as did his listeners, Jesus said you can only serve one master; you can only pay your homage to one. Your loyalty must be undivided.

In this instance, Jesus is saying that a person has only two choices in life, to serve God or mammon. One cannot serve two masters. The word mammon is simply the word for property. Jesus did not use this word in an evil sense. Jesus was saying that you cannot serve your possessions by putting them first in life and also have God first in life. Everyone must make a choice.

Jesus often emphasized the principle that no one can follow him with divided loyalties. God must always come first — before family, before prestige and power, before money, before anything else in the world. You cannot serve two masters because if you try to do that, your loyalties will always be divided. When one reads Jesus' teachings, it is seen that time and again he emphasized that material possessions were the greatest hindrance to people finding eternal life. There is nothing else that kept more people from God than the wrong attitude toward money and other material possessions.

On one occasion he declared that it was easier for a camel to go through the eye of a needle than for a rich man to get into heaven. This is a very severe statement, but it shows what a serious matter Jesus considered riches to be in the life of an individual.

When we analyze Jesus' comments on possessions and money matters, it is apparent that Jesus recognized the weakness of possessions. They did not answer the ultimate issues of life. Jesus did not say they were unimportant. He never criticized riches. He emphasized that they must not take first place in life.

On one occasion Jesus said that a person will be wise if he builds the foundations of his life with as much care as a wise housebuilder constructs the foundations under the structure. He told of a successful farmer who could not make a successful life on the abundance of his crops. Life calls for stronger foundations than that. Someone has suggested, "No man has ever succeeded in making a great God out of little gadgets."

One thing is very sure: the floods and storms will surely come. It is then that we discover our true refuge and strength is not in money or other material possessions.

Jesus warned against this just before he made the statement about serving two masters. In the previous paragraph he said, "Do not lay up for yourselves treasures on earth, where moth and rust consume and where thieves break in and steal, but lay up for yourselves treasures in heaven, where neither moth nor rust consumes and where thieves do not break in and steal; for where your treasure is, there will your heart be also" (Matthew 6:19-21). Again and again Jesus warned people of the fundamental weakness of over-valuing material possessions.

Some live by the slogan, "Your purse is your best friend." This is a great fallacy. It is nice for parents to know that they have provided economic security for their family, but if they are wise, they know that the dike is still full of leaks. A great fortune is often insufficient to buy even one more hour of life. You can't take it with you!

Frugality, thrift, and industry are fine virtues, but any person who has nothing more than these, fine as they are, may still be impoverished and helpless in his hour of great need. It can happen that a person who has spent a great deal of energy amassing a fortune may find that in a crisis one's money has cost too much. One's soul may be lost.

When Jesus was tempted in the wilderness at the beginning of his ministry, he was offered "all the kingdoms of the world and the glory of them" (Matthew 4:8). Jesus saw the world cannot be saved by the compounding of power or possessions, no matter how attractive they may seem. If this were true, salvation would have come long ago through the fortunes and power of the great conquerors who brought millions to their knees. Jesus recognized the weakness of possessions at the outset of his ministry. He saw that possessions can only give creature comforts. That is why he said that people need more than bread; they need bread, but they need much more.

Also, Jesus pointed out that Christians must be different from the rest of the world in their attitudes toward material possessions. This involves how we spend money and how much is given to God. Anyone who has truly had an experience of Christ, who has been born again, who has been transformed by Christ, is a different person. If one is committed to Christ, one does not look upon one's life as one's own. Rather, such a person belongs to God who controls and rules life. When that happens, God rules all that we have as well because he rules our wills, our motives, our every act.

If we are in Christ, we must serve God and not mammon. Again and again Jesus discussed the question of money in such a way as to make it plain that a Christian will look at his possessions from an entirely different viewpoint than the person with only a this-world outlook.

Christians who rent property will be a different kind of landlord. If they own apartment houses, their stewardship will demand that they are in part responsible for the family life inside the building. It is inconceivable that a Christian who has become a child of God should be indifferent to the fire hazards or health conditions existing in the property he offers for rent.

Many times we attempt to see if people think rightly about religion. Are they orthodox in their theology? There are people who emphasize the new birth, evangelism, and correct theology who are sometimes moral outlaws when it comes to their personal finances and the church. There is a great deal of practical atheism among some who solemnly call themselves Christians. Some talk about defending Christian civilization, at the same time withholding the contributions the church needs to win the world to Christ. There are those who complain about the spread of non-Christian religions at the same time they contribute nothing to missions.

Americans spend less for all Protestant missionary programs in a year than they do for tobacco and cosmetics.

Further, Jesus supported standards of conduct regarding possessions and money matters. Normally, people do not complain about standards, but they often try to forget standards regarding money.

The Old Testament standard that Jesus endorsed was giving to God 10% of one's income. The writer of the book of Malachi quoted the Lord as saying that people were robbing him by not giving to him the full tithes. " 'Bring the full tithes into the storehouse ... and thereby put me to the test,' says the Lord of hosts, 'if I will not open the windows of heaven to you and pour down for you an overflowing blessing' " (Malachi 3:10). In other words, the scriptures look upon the tithe as spiritual. God's blessings will come to the one who tithes.

One time Jesus was upbraiding the scribes and Pharisees for their legalisms. He declared, "You tithe ... and have neglected justice and mercy and faith. These you ought to have done" (Matthew 23:23) without neglecting such things as the tithe. We see that Jesus endorsed the tithe.

Jesus was pointing out that tithes are a part of dedicated religious living, but it was not a legalism. Christians who assume that the grace of Christ excuses them from payment of the tithe in harmony with the ancient tradition have misread the scriptures. Jesus never hinted that this acknowledgment of God's sovereign ownership should not be made.

The tithe is not a method of striking a bargain with God. Any person who interprets the tithe in this way will fail as a good steward. The good steward who gives because of enthusiastic loyalty to the causes in which God is especially interested does not look upon the tithe as a legalism.

Jesus was a good steward. We are told that he placed money in the offerings on occasion and know there were many offerings required in that day. It is highly significant that at his trial, when his opponents were looking for every possible reason to crucify him and bring charges against him, not one person came forth to declare that Jesus was delinquent in his temple dues. Nor did anyone say he had failed to pay his taxes to Caesar. Such testimony would have been very damaging evidence in Pilate's court if it could have been produced. Jesus was very careful in his handling of money.

There are people who say they cannot figure how much their tithes are. One person confided to another, "I am not exactly sure what my income is." The friend suggested, "Suppose that God should offer to give you an increase of 10% on this year's income. How would you figure it? If you know a way to get an additional 10%, you should be able to figure out what you ought to give as 10%."

The true tither does not give his tenth for the purpose of bribing God to provide him with prosperity. One who has caught the vision of stewardship gives his tithe in recognition that God is the owner of everything and that man is his steward, responsible for the management and administration of that which God has committed to his care. It is an evidence of our recognition of a moral and spiritual relationship that is the most sacred part of a Christian's life.

The basic contribution Jesus made to this question on which he spoke so often was the doctrine of stewardship by which a man is held responsible for his management of money. There can be no general rise in moral values until our attitude toward money is spiritualized. This is as much a spiritual problem as church attendance, prayer life, Bible reading, or any other aspect of life.

If our attitudes toward the Christian faith are a matter of our eternal destiny, our Christian giving cannot be a matter of unconcern, neither to us nor to our Lord. This was a key plank in Jesus' platform.

Chapter 11

Concerning Suffering

I have said this to you, that in me you may have peace. In the world have tribulations; but be of good cheer, I have overcome the world! — John 16:33

One of the greatest problems that the human race faces is that of suffering. Suffering is an enigma. Suffering is an experience that seems to be without any meaning. Thus, we must look beyond our own experiences of suffering in an attempt to find meaning. As Christians we believe that in our faith we must find an answer to all of the problems of life. Therefore, we turn to Christ to see what he has to say to the problem of suffering.

Suffering challenges our beliefs about God. Some suffering can be explained because people break the laws of God. However, often there seems to be nothing rational in suffering insofar as its distribution is concerned, and there is no justice in suffering when the amount of suffering is considered. For these reasons people often come to feel that God is either lacking in goodness or power or both.

Jesus gives us hope in a statement he made to his disciples in the upper room the night prior to his crucifixion. In the conversation with the disciples, he said, "I have said this to you, that in me you may have peace. In the world you have tribulation; but be of good cheer, I have overcome the world" (John 16:33). These were spoken to men who would soon be among those persecuted for their faith. It was a promise that all would not be easy for them. "You will have tribulation."

Most politicians say that if they win, their followers will have good jobs and prosperity will follow. Everyone will have discovered the end of the rainbow. Jesus' promise to his followers did not present a fine future for those he wanted to continue his work and program. He probably could have gotten more support if he had promised them an easy time. The only encouraging note of hope for the future was, "Be of good cheer, I have overcome the world" (John 16:33). In this one sentence we find Jesus giving us something to hold when all the world seems to collapse on us as the disciples thought it was collapsing on them.

Before the upper room experience, Jesus had spoken of suffering. He had actually promised suffering to his followers on earlier occasions. In the Sermon on the Mount, he had said, "Blessed are those who are persecuted for righteousness' sake, for theirs is the kingdom of heaven. Blessed are you when men revile you and persecute you and utter all kinds of evil against you falsely on my account. Rejoice, and be glad, for your reward is great in heaven, for so men persecuted the prophets who were before you" (Matthew 5:10-12).

Later he amplified this promise of suffering when he told his followers, "I send you out as sheep in the midst of wolves" (Matthew 10:16). And, he added, that they would be on trial before councils and be flogged and hauled before the civil authorities for his sake.

It is significant that Jesus did not try to explain away suffering. He accepted it as a fact. On one occasion Jesus was teaching the disciples. Some people to whom he was talking told him that there were some Galileans who had been killed by Pilate during a religious observance. Jesus then asked, "Do you think that these Galileans were worse sinners than all the other Galileans, because they suffered thus?" (Luke 13:2). He then answered his own question, saying, "No." He continued by reminding them that there was a tower, called the tower of Siloam, which had fallen and killed eighteen people. He asked, "Do you think that they were worse offenders than all the others who dwelt in Jerusalem?" (Luke 13:4). Again, he answered his own question, "No."

Jesus was facing a popular interpretation of suffering that had been a part of Jewish thinking for many years. In reading the Old Testament, suffering was often blamed on sins that people supposedly had committed. The best known of these interpretations is found in the book of Job.

Job was physically afflicted in many ways. He sustained great losses in his family. His fortune was destroyed. Some men who presumably were his friends came to him and said these misfortunes came because he had sinned. Job replied that he had not sinned but his friends insisted he must have sinned somehow to be visited with such misfortunes.

This idea was not expressed only in Job. It is found in other portions of the Old Testament, especially in the Psalms.

Jesus inherited these interpretations of suffering from his Jewish background. It is illustrated in Jesus' encounter with the man born blind. The disciples, reflecting Old Testament thought, asked him, "Rabbi, who sinned, this man or his parents, that he was born blind?" (John 9:2). Jesus replied, "It was not this man who sinned, nor his parents, but that the works of God might be manifest in him" (John 9:3). With this Jesus healed the man.

Jesus did not try to explain suffering. He felt that suffering offered an opportunity to glorify God. He wants us to use our sufferings as a door of opportunity to witness to his grace. We can do this, he assures us, because suffering can be redemptive and victorious for those who look beyond the immediate adversities of life.

In speaking to his disciples in Jerusalem the last week before his death, Jesus told them that there would be great tribulations and sufferings in the world. He predicted that nation would rise against nation, that people would experience earthquakes, pestilences, famines, terrors, and that they would be persecuted by those who opposed the gospel. Then, he said, "This will be a time for you to bear testimony" (Luke 21:13). He told them they would be divided from their families because of him, and added, "By your endurance you will gain your lives" (Luke 21:19).

Through the experiences of suffering and adversity they would have the opportunity to bear testimony for God and the faith. Paul endorsed such a philosophy as he interpreted Christ to the pagan world. In his first letter to the church at Corinth, Paul tells how Christians were made a spectacle to the world. In the Greek, the word meaning "spectacle" is *theatron*. Paul was making an analogy between the amphitheater of that day in which the gladiators fought and in which the Christians were often killed. He pictured himself and other Christians as being in the amphitheater of life and suffering before the world. He is saying that those who do this with faith in God look above and beyond the amphitheater into the eternities. Often we think of ourselves as only spectators, but suffering is so certain that everyone will be in an amphitheater of his own at some time. In these inevitable sufferings we will have the opportunity to bear witness to our own ability to see purpose in our sufferings. "This will be a time for you to bear testimony."

Not only does Jesus suggest that sufferings are an opportunity to bear testimony and witness, he also suggests that our sufferings should be made redemptive. We have cited above that he said the man born blind was in that condition so that God could be glorified. More than anything Jesus said was his own example in which he showed the glory of God and the fact that adversity and tribulation could be made redemptive. It was on the cross that Jesus spoke — not just in words, but more eloquently — in the very fact of the crucifixion.

Jesus never blamed nature and the creation of God for the troubles of people. While his attitude toward the sufferings of others makes up much of the known story of his life on earth, it is well to remember that Christ himself suffered and died on the cross. When we look at his sufferings on the cross, we see one who showed himself divine in the way he suffered and by his victory over that suffering. Christ's suffering was more than just physical suffering, as horrible as that was. He was suffering for the sins of humans, and those sorrows were undoubtedly a greater suffering for him than the outward physical torture.

On the cross, Jesus showed that God bears our sufferings and sorrows. The trials of people have been taken by God upon himself. This is illustrated on the human plane in a statement of Abraham Lincoln to a friend, "I have not suffered by the South, I have suffered with the South. Their pain has been my pain; their loss has been my loss."

Many times in history, there have been those who identified themselves with the sufferings of others. Because of this identification, they themselves have suffered. When this happens, it is not said that their lives are failures, but that they have reached the zenith of purposeful living. There is a plaque in the chapel of Peking Union Medical College in memory of Dr. Hall who died of the plague while attending his patients. On it is a statement a patient made of him, "He took my sickness into his own heart."

God shows through the life of Christ that he bears our sufferings and sins. The cross points the way to God. It is on the cross as nowhere else that we find the love of God supremely illustrated. Many people are troubled that the love demonstrated on the cross is such a costly love. The question that confronts us is whether there can be such a thing as love if it does not cost the lover something. Love can only be understood by its degree of sacrifice, otherwise it would only be a meaningless sentiment. The love of God as seen in Christ and the Christlike love shown by one person to another is always a costly love. It can be no other way.

Jesus chose the cross and the crown of victory followed. Too often people want the victory but reject the cross which first is necessary if one is to have the crown.

H. Wheeler Robinson relates a conversation he had. "I asked a Christian man who had suffered through many years with little or no hope of escape from the physical pain, what his suffering meant to him. He thought a little and then said, 'Well, it seems as if one came up against a blank wall, with no way through, and then — a door opens.' I said, 'And what is the key that opens the door?' 'Ah,' he replied, 'God has the key to that.' "

People suffer from a variety of afflictions. This does not mean those troubles are removed from the concern of God. Faith teaches that every event, no matter how disastrous, is controlled by the purposes of God and can be interpreted only in the light of the divine love from which nothing can separate us.

In the upper room Jesus promised his disciples tribulation, but they should be of good cheer. Why could he promise them that? If one turns to the previous verse, he declared, "I am not alone, for the Father is with me." Then he added, "I have said this to you, that in me you may have peace," and then added, "In the world you have tribulation, but be of good cheer, I have overcome the world" (John 16:32-33).

In the midst of all the tribulations of life, Jesus gives the clue to victory: Live close to the heavenly Father, find peace through faith in Christ, and be of good cheer in the power of Christ. That is the victory that overcomes the world.

Chapter 12

Concerning Love

This is my commandment, that you love one another as I have loved you. — John 15:12

The Christian faith is often described as a religion of love. Children are told that God is love. At an early age, children are taught to sing, "Jesus loves me." Often people speak of love, even Christian love, in a vague manner. To say that God is love seems to be a cliché. Like motherhood and apple pie, people are for love, but what is meant when people say they are for love?

The basis for God's love is found in many places in the scriptures. When we consider the platform of Jesus, it is essential that we search for what Jesus said about love. In the upper room on the night before his death, Jesus told his disciples, "This is my commandment, that you love one another as I have loved you" (John 15:12).

We must always keep in mind that Christian love is an involved love. The non-Christian world has been unable to accept Christ for many reasons. Many cannot believe in a God who became involved in the world of people with their sins and problems.

In the seventeenth century, a philosophical movement known as deism became prominent. Basically a deist believes that God or something started the world spinning, and then withdrew. If there is a personal God, he has withdrawn from any involvement in the world. The Christian believes God created the world, but has not left it. He is interested in the world, showing his continual involvement by sending Christ. He shows his continuing presence through the Holy Spirit.

John 3:16 has radical implications. God so loved the world that he sent his Son. God became involved. His involvement was motivated by love. That one sentence is the Christian answer to deism.

There are people who gladly accept the fact that God became involved in the world. Yet, when the church of Christ becomes involved in the cause of peace, justice, and human rights, those same people say the church should stick to "religion." They appear to desire a monastic faith safe from any involvement with the affairs of the world. These same people fail to remember that the ancient psalmist said of God and his creation of man, "Thou hast made him [man] little less than God ... thou hast placed all things under his feet" (Psalm 8:5-6). If we accept this biblical view of humanity, any degradation of man is an insult to God. That is why the church must be involved in the issues of life.

It must be remembered that when Christ came, he was involved in some of the fundamental problems of his day. Jesus was controversial toward the established religion and the government of his day. Both looked upon him as a threat, and for that reason they wanted to destroy him.

The Christian message of love has been repeated so often that many people look on it in a ho-hum way. Yet, it is this lack of love that has a degrading effect on people. For example, widows and widowers, those who have lost a spouse, are among those who need love. It is such people who should be invited to dinner on occasion. Those who invite them are showing practical, Christian, love to those experiencing loneliness.

A boy entered a church building in a Midwestern city. On a little used stairway, he lighted a candle that set the church building on fire, causing extensive damage. Eventually, the boy was apprehended. Rather than pursue vindictive action toward the boy, the congregation, in spite of its loss, paid for psychiatric help for the boy.

In the upper room Jesus spoke of love. Then he told the disciples to go and bear fruit. But, he added, you will be hated and persecuted because of this. People are not persecuted except that they are involved in controversy. As long as the church is complacent, as long as pastors preach a milk-toast religion, all is well. But when it is shown that love demands involvement in the ghettos where people are held down so they cannot live to the highest levels of their potential, the issue of God's love becomes controversial to many. Such involvement becomes anathema.

Jesus shows us that love must be personalized. Incarnation is the act of God taking human form. In the upper room Jesus commanded people to love "as I have loved you."

Involvement in personalized love is the acceptance of people as they are. Too often we categorize people by saying we love them if they conform to our mores or standards. If they do not, we will have nothing to do with them. The worst of sinners must be accepted. The purpose of the church is to make a saint from a sinner.

Many years ago, a man ran for the presidency of the United States. For years, he had been a member of one political party. When he was being considered the candidate of the other party, he changed parties and won the nomination of that party. (He did not win the election.) When a staunch member of the party that had nominated the man complained about the man changing parties to win the nomination, someone asked him, "Don't you believe in conversion?" The staunch party member replied, "Of course, but when the street woman joins the church, I don't want her singing in the choir the next Sunday."

There are too many in the church who have that attitude; they do not want to accept people fully without first trying to make them conform to the standards of the so-called establishment members. Acceptance is always qualified.

If we are love as Jesus loved, "as I have loved you," we must accept people and love them, even those perceived to be unloveable. This must not be done in the abstract, but in the life issues and relationships of this world.

If we are to love as Jesus loved, it must always be a sacrificial love. The woman who had been ill for years only touched the hem of his garment to be healed. When she did this, Jesus was aware that power had left him. He was sacrificing his own energy for another. Love is always costly. If it does not cost, it is not love.

This is the love of which he spoke when he said that one could have no greater love than when one gives his life for others. Jesus' love meant the giving of his life on the cross.

Mary Cornwell-Legh, an English woman of some means, had visited India in 1915 and had seen work among lepers. When she reached Japan, she went to Kusatsu, a leper colony. What she saw caused her to cancel her ticket home. Instead, she used her own money to work there. She and her colleagues bought land and built, year by year, a cluster of homes, known as St. Barnabas. This included men's and women's as well as children's residences. She became a mother and friendly counselor to the lepers. Later, the Episcopal church helped.

When Mary Cornwell-Legh first arrived, what was known as the Lower Village was the home of nearly 900 lepers. It was called the Valley of Gehenna because there was so much suffering, anguish, grief, and despair. There was an average of about six suicides a week.

It became no longer the Valley of Gehenna, but the Garden of Prayer. About two-thirds of the people became Christians. After Miss Cornwell-Legh had been in the leper village for a few years, there were only two suicides in two years, for she brought love, encouragement, and hope.

Too often churches seem to think more of themselves than of the world. The administrative board of a congregation was discussing its program. One member of the board commented that nearly everything the congregation did was directed for its own benefit. He questioned its priorities.

It is always in order for a congregation to analyze where its money goes and how it is used. How much has been invested in its buildings? How much is needed for the maintenance of the buildings? Yet, many church facilities are used only a few hours a week. In the meantime they are cleaned, they are heated, but often stand idle for days.

Is this good Christian stewardship? Is our investment in buildings that are used minimally the kind of sacrifice for others to which Christ calls us? Do our total church programs indicate we are showing Christ's love to the world? Whether we are thinking of Christ's command to love as individuals or as congregations, such love must be directed toward others in a sacrificial manner.

Chapter 13

Concerning Life After Death

Did I not tell you that if you would believe you would see the glory of God? — John 11:40

The issue of life after death has faced mankind from its beginning. It is a problem that is still with us. Jesus did not avoid the issue as he spoke of eternal life.

How can one face life victoriously and how can one face death victoriously? The two questions are closely related; they cannot be separated.

Like every other issue, Jesus speaks to the problem of death because it is one every person faces and will ultimately experience. In the scriptures we find the story about the death of Lazarus, the brother of Mary and Martha. The sisters had sent word to Jesus, telling him that their brother was very ill. However, Jesus did not go immediately to Bethany. Rather, he waited two days. It was then that Jesus returned to Judea and walked to the village of Bethany, on the Mount of Olives, east of Jerusalem. On his way to Bethany, he told his disciples that Lazarus was dead and he was glad he had not been there to heal him because what was going to happen would help strengthen their belief in him. When he arrived at Bethany, he was told Lazarus had been in the tomb for four days. After talking to Mary and Martha, Jesus went to the tomb.

To picture this, one must remember the typical Palestinian tomb. Many times the tombs were either natural caves or were cut into the rock. The tomb consisted of an entrance beyond which were shelves, usually three on each side and two on the wall that faced the entrance. The bodies were laid on these shelves. After death, the bodies were swathed in bandage-like wrappings, and the head was wrapped with a towel. The tomb had no door, but in front there was a great stone, like a cartwheel. This stone was rolled across the entrance so that the tomb was sealed.

Jesus asked that the stone be moved. Martha could only think of one reason for opening the tomb — that Jesus wished to look on the face of his dead friend for the last time. Martha could see no consolation in that. What consolation could anyone gain from looking on the grim and repulsive sight of a putrefying corpse?

She pointed out that Lazarus had been in the tomb for four days. This was a reference to the Jewish belief that the spirits of the departed hovered around the tombs for four days, seeking an entrance again into the body of the dead. But, after four days, the spirits left, for the face of the body was so decayed that no one could recognize it.

It was in that situation and setting that Jesus said to Martha, "Did I not tell you that if you would believe you would see the glory of God?" (John 11:40). With that Jesus lifted his eyes toward heaven and prayed that his Father would hear him and that the people would come to believe that he himself had been sent by God. Then he called, "Lazarus, come out" (John 11:43). And Lazarus came from the tomb.

When this happened, the word that Jesus had spoken earlier, upon hearing of Lazarus' illness, came true, that Lazarus was ill "for the glory of God, so that the Son of God may be glorified by means of it" (John 11:4).

When we read the New Testament, we find that Jesus said very little about physical death. On the other hand, he often spoke directly or by implication of spiritual death. In the New Testament we find that Paul wrote more about immortality than the recorded words of Jesus on the same subject. However, the gospel accounts spend a great proportion of time on events centering around the death and resurrection of Jesus.

It is evident from the scriptures that Jesus emphasized eternal life in contrast to the idea of life after death or immortality. In some education materials for young people the question is asked, "What is eternal life?" The correct answer is, "Eternal life is that sweet fellowship which a Christian has with God is this life and is perfected in joy and happiness in the life hereafter."

With this we see that eternal life is in the here and now. It is not something confined to the sweet by and by, after physical death. When one reads the fourth gospel, eternal life is expressed many times. Most of the times it refers to the life we are experiencing here and now. In chapter 5 of John the words of Jesus are recorded, "For as the Father raises the dead and gives them life, so also the Son gives life ... I say to you, he who hears my word and believes him who sent me, has eternal life; he does not come into judgment, but has passed from death to life" (John 5:21, 24). It is significant that Jesus used the word has — using the present tense. Eternal life or heaven is a continuance or expansion of a quality of life already imparted to the person who believes in Christ and follows his way.

When Jesus asked the disciples if they were going to leave him, Peter said they had nowhere else to go because Jesus said to his followers, "My sheep hear my voice, and I know them, and they follow me; and I give them eternal life, and they shall never perish" (John 10:27-28).

Prior to Christ's death and resurrection, a man known as the rich young ruler came to Jesus asking what he must do to inherit eternal life. Jesus told him to sell his possessions; Jesus was associating eternal life with stewardship. What is done with life and possessions is a mark of eternal life today as well as in Jesus' day.

In addition, the ethical demands of eternal life are emphasized by Paul in his first letter to Timothy when he declared that Christians are to "do good, to be rich in good deeds, liberal and generous, thus laying up for themselves a good foundation for the future, so that they may take hold of the life which is life indeed" (1 Timothy 6:18-19).

We must also remember that eternal life is a quality that depends on one's conversion and commitment to Christ. We are again reminded of the rich young ruler who refused to commit himself and his treasures to God and went away sorrowful because he did not obtain the eternal life he desired.

In the parable of the judgment, Jesus said that those who lacked the commitment necessary to use their possessions generously were denied life with God after death.

Dr. Robert McAfee Brown tells an incident in which the story of Jesus raising Lazarus played a leading part in the transformation of life. Dr. Brown was an army chaplain and was on a troopship in which 1,500 Marines were returning from Japan to the United States for discharge after World War II. He was approached by a group of Marines who asked him to study the Bible with them. He leaped at the opportunity. Near the end of the voyage they were studying chapter 11 of John. After they had studied it, a Marine came to Dr. Brown. "Everything in that chapter," he said, "is pointing at me." He continued to say he had been in hell for the previous six months. He had gone straight into the Marines from college. He had been sent to Japan. He had been bored with life; he had gotten into trouble — real trouble. Nobody knew about it, but God knew. He felt guilty. He felt his life was ruined; he felt he could never face his family although they need never know. He felt he had killed himself and was a dead man. "And," he said, "after reading this chapter I have come alive again." Then he added, "I know that this resurrection Jesus was talking about is real here and now, for he has raised me from death to life."

This young man truly came to believe. He experienced the power of God in life. His troubles were not finished. He had a hard row ahead. But in his sin and his sense of guilt he had found Jesus as the resurrection and the life. His new commitment, his sense of dependence on the grace of God, were manifestations of the glory of God. The question Jesus asked Martha was relevant in the Marine's life: "Did I not tell you that if you would believe, you would see the glory of God?" (John 11:49). Only when this Marine was converted and committed himself to God through Christ did he find eternal life. Like the prodigal son, it could be said of him that he had been dead but now was alive when he returned to the Father.

Finally, life with God after death is a promise to those who are in Christ. He raised Lazarus as he had also raised the daughter of Jairus and the son of the widow of Nain. He said that there was life with God after they experienced physical death. The real barrier to life with God was spiritual death and that took place on this side of physical death.

In the upper room on the night before his own death, he told his disciples, "In my Father's house are many rooms; if it were not so, would I have told you that I go to prepare a place for you" (John 14:2). This was the assurance that through his death he was providing a place in heaven for his faithful followers and giving them the assurance at the same time that there was a place for them provided by God. He continued by declaring that because he lived and would live after death, his disciples would also live after death.

Here is one of the paradoxes of the Christian faith: that eternal life is both the quality of living on this side of physical death and at the same time is life with God after we pass through the doorway of death. This is experienced by those who live, using the phrase of Paul, "in Christ," by those to whom Christ is real in their own experience.

This was the thought of Jesus when he declared that he was the true vine and that those who follow him are branches of that vine. It must be remembered that he said the branches must bear fruit in order to prove they are his disciples.

In what is called the high priestly prayer of Jesus as recorded in the upper room experience, Jesus said, "This is eternal life, that they know thee the only true God, and Jesus Christ whom thou hast sent" (John 17:3). How does a person know him? One who believes in him and commits himself to him will see the glory of God. It is a glory that one will share with him when one allows Christ to live in one's life through full commitment. This glory shall be shared in this life with God. It is also Christ's promise for the life after death. It is the glory manifested in raising Lazarus and in his other great acts. It is a glory shown by God in Christ's resurrection. Any person who believes these things shall see the glory of God as Martha did.

Chapter 14

Concerning The First Coming Of Christ

For the Son of man came to seek and to save that which was lost. — Luke 19:10

You shall call his name Jesus, for he will save his people from their sins. — Matthew 1:21

For to you is born this day ... a Savior, who is the Christ the Lord. — Luke 2:11

During political campaigns candidates are interviewed by the media. One question often asked of presidential candidates is, "Why do you want to be president?" As one might expect, the answers are varied. Yet, each candidate seems to imply that he has certain qualifications which would enable him to meet the problems of the world.

Jesus, too, made statements in which he claimed to be qualified for the commitment that he desires people would make to him as the leader of life. He told the disciples that if they followed him, he would make them "fishers of men." On various occasions he said that he was one with the Father, that he had come from the Father.

Jesus' claims that he was qualified in this manner are much more profound that anything found in the statements of political candidates in our day. It is interesting that one of the deepest and most all-embracing statements of Jesus along this line was not made at the beginning of his ministry, but on his last trip to Jerusalem, two weeks before the crucifixion. It was a sweeping statement of what he could do for people. It was made in the home of Zacchaeus with whom he was having dinner. After Zacchaeus was moved by the presence and spirit of Christ to pledge restoration fourfold to those whom he had defrauded, Jesus told Zacchaeus that salvation had that day come to that house, declaring, "For the Son of Man came to seek and to save that which was lost" (Luke 19:10).

This is the basis of the incarnation. Jesus came to save. Many look upon Jesus as a fine teacher or a very influential person. While these are true, we must not overlook the essentials: Jesus Christ is Savior. He came to save all who are lost.

This was not a claim made only by Jesus. Matthew records that the angel, speaking to Joseph before the birth of Jesus, declared, "You shall call his name Jesus, for he will save his people from their sins" (Matthew 1:21). Later the angels gave the shepherds the good news for all people because there was "born this day in the city of David a Savior, who is Christ the Lord" (Luke 2:11).

That is the reason Christians celebrate Christmas. It marks the birth of a Savior. This is the message for all people. A Savior has come!

It seems that everyone celebrates Christmas. Rich man, poor man, beggar man, thief, all observe the day. Doctor, lawyer, merchantman, chief, all remember.

One can visit large department stores in Tokyo in November and listen to Christmas carols over the public address systems in a country that is primarily Shinto-Buddhist. In homes of Buddhists and Muslims in the United States, one might find Christmas trees. All give gifts and exchange the season's greetings. Faithful adherents of all religions keep the Christmas season. There is, however, a great difference between celebrating with tinsel and observing the birth of a Savior.

No matter what the inclinations of people, all need help with the fundamental problems of life. Paul, in his epistle to the Romans, painted a terrifying word picture of the vice, perversion, cruelty, and inhumanity of a world that knows no Savior (ch. 1:18-32). But a Savior did come to a needy world. That is what the Christian church proclaims each December: There is a great joy for all people, a Savior who is Christ the Lord!

It is the hope of every pastor as he or she looks over the congregation on Christmas that the presence of the gathered community is *prima facie* evidence that the parishioners have found Christ as Savior. He came to save us from sin, from fear, from selfishness, from the sting of death. Many seem in a vague way to want Jesus as Savior, but hardly know what his salvation means or demands.

Amid the tinsel of the Christmas season and the oft-repeated singing of "Rudolph, The Red-Nosed Reindeer," Christians are called to believe the messengers of God who proclaim the Savior. The accounts in both the gospels of Matthew and Luke are stories of those who did believe the messages they received. One story tells of shepherds to whom the angels appeared in those fields east of Bethlehem. When the angels had made the announcement, "The shepherds said to one another, 'Let us go over to Bethlehem and see this thing that has happened' " (Luke 2:15). There was no doubt in the minds of the shepherds; they believed the message that God sent.

The gospel written by Matthew tells of the wise men. God spoke to them in a different way than he spoke to the shepherds. When the wise men followed the star, they found the Christ. Neither shepherds or wise men would have found the Savior if they had not believed the messages and signs of God.

Among the legends of Marco Polo is a Christmas story. According to the tradition, each of the three wise men set out to follow the star with great hopes. Each was looking for a different thing. Gaspar, the youngest, had a strong feeling that the world needed a ruler, so he hoped to find a Lord. Balthasar, the second, was conscious of a growing spiritual dullness, an inner lack in his life, so he hoped the star would lead him to God. Melchior, the eldest, however, felt another kind of need. He had the feeling of guilt on his conscience, and he hoped to find cleansing.

All of them were disappointed when they reached the stable and saw only a peasant woman and a baby. As they turned to leave, they heard Mary sing, "My soul magnifies the Lord." "The Lord," said Gaspar, and turned back. Mary continued the song, "And my spirit rejoices in God my Savior." At the sound of the word "God," Balthasar's eyes lighted with excitement, and he turned back into the stable. Then, at the end of the phrase, Mary mentioned "Savior." A Savior! That was exactly for what Melchior was looking. So he, too, turned back eagerly to the stable.

This, of course, is only a legend, based on the Christmas story recorded in the third gospel, but it expresses in imaginative form the profound truth of the incarnation. The babe in the manger, when he grew up, in his life and death and resurrection, brought to the world those three great gifts for which the wise men were looking. He brought the revelation of God. He brought cleansing and forgiveness of sins and the power to overcome sin. He brought a ruler to the world. Likewise, we, too, must believe the Christ to be God, Ruler, and a Savior.

When we believe this message of God, good tidings of great joy can ring in our time, and life can be different for us, even in the twenty-first century. If we believe the babe of Bethlehem as the Christ, as our Savior, we can go beyond Christmas with light in our hearts, with confidence and courage, no matter what life brings.

It should be our hope that Christmas brings us to Christ as it did the shepherds. The shepherds returned to their fields, but with a newness in their lives, for now they were glorifying and praising God for what they had heard and seen. We, too, can now go endlessly through the valleys and shadows, if we place our lives against the background of the everlasting love that holds life together.

This is what a child inadvertently suggested when he went out at the end of January to sing carols. A householder, listening to the strains of "Hark, The Herald Angels Sing" opened the door and asked, "Don't you know Christmas was a month ago?" "Yes, sir," said the singing boy, "but I had the flu then and couldn't go caroling." It is time for caroling any time if we know what the shepherds knew.

Further, we must remember that if we are to be partakers in God's salvation, we must commit our lives to him in every act. The shepherds would never have found a Savior if they had not acted on the message that came to them. The wise men never would have found the one whom they came so many miles to see.

Not only did the shepherds act in coming to the manger. The glorious thing is that "they made known the saying which had been told them concerning [the] child" (Luke 2:17). The shepherds returned to their fields glorifying and praising God. So convincing were they that those who heard it wondered at what the shepherds told them.

The wise men, too, acted. When they came into the presence of Christ, they fell down and worshiped him. Then opening their treasures, they offered him gifts, gold, frankincense, and myrrh. These were costly treasures.

When we examine the reactions of the shepherds and the wise men, it is apparent that Christ is only a Savior if we combine the elements of praise and worship on one hand and the giving and commitment of life on the other. Because of Jesus, the Christian faith is a giving religion. It begins with God. "God so loved the world that he gave ..." (John 3:16).

How about us? How much do we love Christ? Our salvation depends not only on a vague belief in Christ, but also on our gifts to others in Christ's name, on our commitment of life and possessions to Christ. Like the shepherds, all Christians are to proclaim the coming of Christ. Like the wise men, we are here to dedicate our possessions for Christ.

A mountain climber invited a companion to scale the summit of a towering peak with him. As they sat together on the top of the mountain, with a beautiful panorama below, the guest saw the other man weeping. He asked, "Why are you crying?" The reply came back, "All these years I have come here alone and filled my soul with the cup of God. Today, I am happier than I have ever been, for this is the first time I have shared the glory with someone else."

It is sometimes hard to believe that so much of the world is still so far from Christ, even after more than 2,000 years. Many people's ideas are still at cross-purposes with Christ and Christmas. The dedicated Christian, who really claims Christ as Savior, will act on his conviction. One can share him with others, one can commit himself anew to joining the wise men of all ages who have laid before him their very best treasures. With the shepherds one will proclaim to others the message that the world has a Savior.

Dr. Frank Laubach once told of visiting a hydroelectric plant in Liberia. There was a huge pipe and four great turbine wheels. Though the pipe was open above, the wheels were not turning. When asked the reason, the manager said that the pipe was closed at the outlet and unless both the outlet and the inlet were open, the turbines could not run. Dr. Laubach commented, "That is the way our lives are. The pipe must be open up toward God and open down toward man."

Christians should realize and experience that God has opened the channels of his love and concern downward toward us. It is tragic that often we turn off the channels of our hearts and minds so that we cannot feel his power. Yet, wise men and shepherds give us the clue of receiving this power and joy. Like them, we must believe that this is God's event in history and we must act upon it with committed lives. Only then does Christ become your Savior.

Chapter 15

Concerning The Second Coming Of Christ

They asked him, "Lord, will you at this time restore the kingdom to Israel?" He said to them, "It is not for you to know times or seasons which the Father has fixed by his own authority." —Acts 1:6-7

From time to time one reads in the newspapers of some person who has announced that on a certain day the world will come to an end. Or, such a person may say that at a particular time the Lord will return in a dramatic way. Sometimes those who followed such heralds have sold all their property so they would be unencumbered by any material possessions on the great day that is to come.

In July 1960, Mount Blanc in France was the scene of a remarkable ceremony. Members of a religious group camped high on the mountain to await the end of the world that their leaders had forecast for 2:45 p.m. on July 14. As the time approached, women began to scream, and a Tyrolean wearing leather shorts began blowing a bugle that represented the trumpet of doom. This lasted for about a minute; then the leader of the Doomsday cult, Dr. Elio Bianca, an Italian pediatrician, announced, "We made a mistake." The *New York Times* reported the fiasco under the headline, "World Fails to End."

Many people are acquainted with those who spend their time traveling from door to door preaching that the end of the world is imminent, claiming that only those who believe as they do will be saved.

Many of these people base their beliefs on one particular passage in the Bible. These people fail to see that most do not go to the book of Genesis for scientific knowledge regarding the beginnings of the world; it is equally absurd to base all our thoughts of the end of the age on one small passage near the end of the Bible.

People with this thought pattern feel that there is no human remedy for the evil in the world. They believe that only the intervention of God can remedy the chaos of the world with his destructive power at Armageddon. It is well to remember, however, that the word Armageddon appears only once in the Bible, in Revelation 16:16. The writer is describing the place where the last decisive battle is to be fought on the day of judgment; the name may suggest the region around Megiddo where several important Old Testament battles had been fought.

In the twenty-first century, thoughts of how and when Christ will return have come to the forefront in the thought of many Christians because of wars and the devastating effects of those wars. Many have concluded that human efforts are hopeless and only the dramatic intervention of Christ can remedy the evil of the world. Those who hold these views do not, it must be emphasized, draw a blueprint of Christ's return as do some of the fringe sects of America.

The Christian faith is one of expectation and anticipation. In one of Jesus' parables, the woman not only persisted in her search, but she actually found the lost coin. There is a lesson in his story of the woman who beat her knuckles raw on the unyielding door, but she eventually awakened the judge and obtained justice. If one was to dismiss the idea of Christ's return, we would find these tireless women — sweeping, sweeping, sweeping or knocking, knocking, knocking — through endless ages of eternity, and accomplishing nothing.

Those who look for this great and dramatic intervention of God are not unique in history. Knowledge of biblical history shows that one of the hopes of the Hebrew people was that God would dramatically intervene and save the nation. In the second century before Christ the Jews experienced the Maccabaean wars that eventually, in 143 BC, freed the Jewish state from foreign domination, a freedom that lasted until 63 BC, when the Roman legions came. Before they attained their freedom, the Jews hoped and hoped for God's intervention as they had done for centuries. This hope was especially pitiful and intense during the period of religious persecutions from about 180 BC to 143 BC. It was in this period that much was written, including the book of Daniel, to encourage the Jews to hold to their faith.

These longings for God's intervention were also prevalent at the time of Jesus. He brought what people perceived in him as hope for a political victory. Then Christ was crucified. That brought great disappointment to the disciples and the general populace. With his resurrection, however, their hopes also rose for they now expected him to use his power to bring about the kingdom that they still perceived as an earthly kingdom.

Luke, the author of not only the gospel account that bears his name, but also the book of Acts, wrote that after Jesus' resurrection he appeared and spoke to them about the kingdom of God. They still did not understand. They asked him, "Lord, will you at this time restore the kingdom to Israel?" They reflected popular thought that looked for the divine intervention in a forceful and dramatic way. Jesus answered them, "It is not for you to know times or seasons which the Father has fixed by his own authority" (Acts 1:7).

The confusion perpetuated by some religious groups is because some claim to have an inside track to the mind of God by which they predict what and how God will bring about the kingdom and to conquer the presence of evil in the world. The apostles thought Jesus would do it with an army. The answer Jesus gave to the disciples is applicable today: "It is not for you to know times or seasons which the Father has fixed by his own authority" (Acts 1:7).

It cannot be ignored that Jesus often spoke of his return. The parable of the talents was told to impress his followers that when he returned, he would expect them to have shown good stewardship.

The relevance of this is obvious. Speculation concerning the return of Christ is often discussed. The return of Christ has always been discussed in times of crisis in life, which threatens despair over the outlook for human history. Augustine and Luther, each at some point in his career, was firmly convinced that the evil age in which he dwelt could not outlast his lifetime — Christ would surely return to end history.

Luke reports Jesus telling his disciples, "There will be signs in sun and moon and stars, and upon the earth distress of nations in perplexity at the roaring of the sea and the waves, men fainting with fear and with foreboding of what is coming on the world; for the powers of the heavens will be shaken. And then they will see the Son of man coming in a cloud with power and great glory" (Luke 21:25-27).

One of the familiar parables of Jesus is that of the wise and foolish bridesmaids in which those who did not prepare their lamps found that they were shut out of the festivities when the bridegroom arrived, a story which parallels the coming of Christ and those who will be unprepared to welcome him.

In his first letter to the church at Thessalonica which was written about the year 51 and is considered by some to be the earliest book of the New Testament, Paul emphasized his belief that Christ would soon return. After that Paul seems to emphasize the idea of Christ's return less and less while he, Paul, was living. That Paul was wrong as to the time when Christ will return does not cancel the idea that he will appear again. Paul, however, does give a bit of astute advice, even though he does seem to proclaim Christ's imminent return, as he said "the day of the Lord will come like a thief in the night" (1 Thessalonians 5:2).

This suggests that Christ's first coming was a surprise. Anyone who was among the wise men of the world in that day would certainly have felt that any Christ who was coming to save the world would come in an important place and in an important way. Some would expect the Christ to come in a place like Rome, which was the political capital of the world. Or, perhaps the Christ could come in Athens, which was the cultural capital of the world, with its tradition of great philosophers.

Others would expect the Savior of the world to come from Alexandria, the educational capital of the world with its great university. Or, in Jerusalem, the religious center, recognized as such by people of many cultural backgrounds. Instead, the Christ appeared in Bethlehem. That was the least likely place for him to appear. Likewise, it is not for us to know the time and place in which Christ will reappear, whether soon or at the climax of history. If Christ's first coming was a surprise, his second coming will probably also be a surprise as to time and place and means.

There are some people who feel that all they have to do is to sit back and wait for the return of the Lord. Jesus indicated, however, he wants us ready whenever he does return. There is no indication that in the meantime he would have people sit and twiddle their thumbs. It is well to remember that God does not work in the crises of history; he also works in the processes of history. No one should wait for him to make a grand appearance in some great crisis.

Jesus indicated to disciples that it was not for them to know when God would set up the kingdom. He had said, "It is not for you to know times or seasons which the Father has fixed by his own authority." Then he continued, "But you shall receive power when the Holy Spirit has come upon you; and you shall be my witness in Jerusalem and in all Judea and Samaria and to the end of the earth" (Acts 1:8).

This means that our work is cut out for us. It means that the touching of life by the Holy Spirit is both a necessity and a promise. When that occurs, something will happen to the Christian. The power of the Holy Spirit will enable us to do God's work here. That work is to witness from a local community to the ends of the world.

Luke records that John the Baptist told the crowds that claiming to be of Jewish heritage was not sufficient, that they must "bear fruits that befit repentance" (Luke 3:8). The people asked him what this meant. He told them to share their material substance with the needy. Tax collectors should not take more than was allowed by law, and soldiers should abstain from violence and not make false accusations against anyone. John declared that charity, justice, and righteousness were requisites for the first coming of Christ; those who prepare for the second coming of Christ must do the same.

In the conversation of Jesus and his disciples as recorded in Acts, it is important to note the sequence of what he was saying: You are trying to probe the mind of God for things that are not your business. But you do have a business, a challenge. Wait until the Holy Spirit has come into your lives. Then you will have so much to do that you will not have to speculate about my return or how God is going to enforce his kingdom. Your task is to witness to my power everywhere in the world.

Jesus never gave his disciples a blueprint of the kingdom. Neither did he give a blueprint of the end of the age or tell of the specific manner of his return. The Christian faith is not a diagram of the end of the ages, but a faith in the Christ of the ages. The Christian's task is to witness to this Christ.

The threat of atomic warfare and other types of social disintegration find many people trembling about ultimate disaster. They wish God would intervene to save the righteous. The time and means that he will use are beyond our knowledge. In the meantime, it is well to remember the attitude of a man when the world seemed to be threatened with what seemed to be ultimate disaster.

On May 19, 1780, during the anxious days of the Revolutionary War that darkness came at noon. Bats flew and chickens roosted. A meteorological phenomenon seemed to bring day to an end when the sun was at its zenith. Panic broke out, and many thought the end of the world was at hand.

At Hartford, Connecticut, the state legislature was in session and, when darkness came at noon, the meeting of the lower house broke up in alarm. In the state senate a motion for adjournment was made, so that the legislators could meet the day of judgment with whatever courage they could muster.

The motion to adjourn was opposed by Abraham Davenport, a Yankee selectman and judge who was a friend and advisor of George Washington. Davenport faced the panic about the end of the world with the best of Yankee heart and head. He arose and addressed his legislative colleagues, "I'm against this adjournment," he said. Then he explained his position: "The day of judgment is either approaching or it is not. If it is not, there is no cause for adjournment. If it is, I choose to be found doing my duty. I wish, therefore, that candles be brought."

Whenever the world has been threatened by disaster people have looked for the intervention of God. There are many who want such intervention today. However, Abraham Davenport gives us an example for times like these. When people are haunted by doubts and threatened with disastrous warfare and the seeming collapse of moral values and are undecided what to do, Jesus would have us be his witnesses. Abraham Davenport suggests the only possible answer, "I choose to be found doing my duty."

Chapter 16

How Do You Vote?

So there was a division among the people over him.
— John 7:43

Every four years we select a president. For months prior to the election we are bombarded by advertisements telling why people should vote for one candidate or the other. After all the visual and auditory bombardment, everyone seems relieved when election day is finally over.

That there is a political campaign means people have an opportunity to choose from a very limited field, the person who shall head the government for the following four years. That there are usually two major candidates, plus several minor ones, means there is a division in the minds of the people as to who will be president.

It is not only in the area of politics that we find a division of opinion. An advertisement in a bus reads, "Yes, you can vote more than once! You vote every time you buy a branded product. You vote for one trademark, reject several others. Manufacturers of branded wares ... welcome this continuous election. It keeps them on their toes, every day, making a variety of the world's finest products to please you. You are the BOSS in this land of brands."

Because of these choices, whether in politics or in what we eat or wear, there is a division of opinion. A division of opinion is nothing new. Jesus experienced a great division of opinion over himself. This conflict among the minds of people is described in chapter 7 of the gospel of John. Often we think we are confused as to whom to follow. It is apparent that this was true in Jesus' day, too.

It was time for the Feast of the Tabernacles. Jesus did not go to Jerusalem immediately for this traditional sacred and important celebration. In those days the festival lasted for eight days.

In chapter 6 of John we are told that many of the followers of Jesus had left him because he did not seem to fulfill their hopes. In the succeeding chapter, Jesus' brothers felt that he had better try to regain popularity and prestige in the eyes of the people. We read that his brothers said to him, "Leave here [Galilee] and go to Judea, that your disciples may see the works you are doing. For no man works in secret if he seeks to be known openly. If you do these things, show yourself to the world" (John 7:3-4).

His brothers did not question that Jesus had great powers, but they believed that he must prove himself in the limelight of the crowds who were gathering at Jerusalem. That was astute political advice. But Jesus told his brothers to go to the feast by themselves. He would not go with them. After they had gone, Jesus went to Jerusalem, not with great fanfare, but privately. At once there was arguing over Jesus. John tells us, "There was much muttering about him among the people. While some said, 'He is a good man,' others said, 'No, he is leading the people astray' " (John 7:12).

The longer Jesus stayed in Jerusalem, the more people learned he was there. By the middle of the feast, he went into the temple and taught. As usual, his teaching was so forceful that people marveled. A discussion arose over the issue of healing on the sabbath. Some began to discuss whether this might be the Christ.

By the last day of the feast, people seemed to be completely confused. John reports that some said this was really a prophet. Others said this was the Christ. There was a debate on the issue because they looked for Christ to come from Judea, not from Galilee. John reports, "So there was a division among the people over him" (John 7:43).

The division among the people over Christ means that people in that day, as well as today have a choice in life. There would be no divisions among the people over candidates today, if there was no choice. In some countries there is no choice. In some nations there is only one candidate and in some places, no vote is even possible.

There are people who surrender their choices to the stars. These are the people who read the astrology columns carried by most daily newspapers in the United States. Those who rely on the "advice" of such columns are living in an easy way. Believing in astrology removes the necessity to think for oneself; the stars do the thinking. If everyone believed in astrology, we would truly have a one-party system. Since no one would have the privilege of thinking for oneself, one could sit back and let the stars rule one's life.

That is not the way life works. We cannot do anything about physical heredity. Most people inherit some of the physical features of their parents or grandparents. No one can do much about that aspect of one's heredity.

There is an aspect of heredity that we can control and about which we have a voice. Someone has called this "choosing our ancestors." While no one can choose his parents, he does have power to choose to follow great minds of the past or those who have been a detriment to the world. No one can choose the bloodstream of life, but people can choose the thought stream.

We have the power to choose to read great literature or trash. In our decisions, we are voting what our family life shall be. The Archbishop of Canterbury once addressed the bride and bridegroom at a prominent wedding: "We all wish you happiness, but our wishes cannot give it. Nor can it come from outward circumstances. It can only come from yourselves, from the spirit that is within you. You cannot choose what changes and chances are to befall you in the coming years. But you can choose the spirit in which you will meet them." Like Joshua, everyone must choose every day whom he will serve. Everyone has choices in life.

Not only do we have choices in life, but we must also learn that there are no split tickets. This is important for those who claim to follow Christ. Jesus emphasized this time and again. He said that whoever put his hand to the plow and looked back was not fit for the kingdom of God. Another time: "Whoever does not bear his own cross and come after me, cannot be my disciple" (Luke 14:27). "If a house is divided against itself, that house will not be able to stand" (Mark 3:25). Further, "He who is not with me is against me, and he who does not gather with me scatters" (Matthew 12:39).

Too many people try to live by voting both ways. Life for many is like that of a skier who tries to ski down a hill, putting a leg on each side of a tree. What is needed is a clear-cut distinction between those who believe in Christ above everything else in the world and those who have no interest in him. Our votes are either "Yes" for Christ or a "No" against him. There is no third alternative.

When people do not vote "Yes," they loose any sense of direction. They become drifters. This is illustrated in one of the best-known novels of the early part of the twentieth century, *Main Street*, by Sinclair Lewis. In the book, Lewis describes the religious state of mind into which one of the town's doctors had drifted. He had continued as a conventional member of the church, without taking it seriously. When his wife finally rebelled at the dullness into which their church life had fallen, the husband was flustered and confused. The author says of him, "He believed in the church but seldom attended its services. He believed in Christianity, but never thought about it. He was worried over his wife's lack of faith, but was not sure just what she lacked." This was a case where not doing anything was a no vote.

Whenever we fail to fight injustice, whenever we tolerate racial prejudices, whenever we take an indifferent attitude toward the homeless and hungry, we are voting no to Christ. How we vote is not just a question that we face on election day; it is a question that faces all Christians every day.

It is important to remember that those who voted yes may not be the apparent winners. Many times one will find himself voting for those who receive a minority of the votes. In our democratic process, we accept the verdict of the majority insofar as, at least in the United States, we do not violently attempt to overthrow the verdict of the majority. However, we must always remember that the majority is not always on the winning side. Those who cast their vote for Christ are always on the winning side.

Chad Walsh was a Midwestern college professor. For many years he voted "no" to Jesus Christ. Eventually he saw the futility of his position. After submitting his life to Christ, he wrote a book, *Stop Looking, and Listen*. In it he called for a clear-cut distinction between those who believe in Christ above everything else in the world and those who have no interest in him. Then Dr. Walsh added:

> *The net result may be that the number of names on the church rolls will be smaller a century from now, but that is a cause for hope, if the professing Christians make up in conviction for what they lack in statistics.*

Christians could never have won a plebiscite in the days when they were almost the only seeds of life in the dying Roman empire.[1]

This gives courage and hope. The history of the Christian faith has not been marked by great majorities. Every time the Christian church tried to extend its power because it controlled a great majority and used that as a means to more power, it became bogged down in what should have been its primary task of redeeming people.

There are times people feel their vote does not count because the issue or person for whom they vote seems lost. Paul gives us a clue to meaning in our vote, even though we find ourselves in the minority. In his letter to the Romans he says "we are more than conquers through Him who loved us" (Romans 8:37). We are winners!

Paul makes this statement after he points out the defeats that we encounter — tribulation, distress, persecution, famine, nakedness, peril, or the sword. In spite of these things, says Paul, we will find ourselves on the winning side if our vote is for Christ in our daily lives.

The committed Christian has confidence that right will ultimately win over wrong. Those who believe in a moral order of the universe as expressed in biblical truths will ultimately be on the winning side. Evil will seem to triumph at times, but God is still the ruler. Christ calls everyone to cast a "Yes" vote for him and his platform.

How do you vote?

---

1. Chad Walsh, *Stop Looking, and Listen* (New York: Harper and Brothers, 1947).

www.ingramcontent.com/pod-product-compliance
Lightning Source LLC
Chambersburg PA
CBHW060847050426
42453CB00008B/880